Arab and

The venerable Jewish evangelist Hyman Appleman was to speak to a conference of Southern Baptist evangelists.

"Shorrosh, come up here," he called from the platform.

Anis (*ah-NEECE*) Shorrosh respectfully complied. Appleman put his arm around the former Palestinian refugee and said, "Brethren, herein is the power of God demonstrated. Only in Christ can Arab and Jew be united."

Then, in the custom of the Middle East, he kissed the younger evangelist. The emotional scene brought tears to participants and onlookers alike as the Arab returned the kiss to the Jew.

How can this be? Palestinian Arab and an old Jew loving one another? Is it possible? It is, for that is the story of THE LIBERATED PALESTINIAN.

The Liberated Palestinian
The Anis Shorrosh Story

James and Marti Hefley

distributed by
ACCLAIMED BOOKS
Box 18186, Dallas, TX 75218
phone (214) 494-2304

Contents

Dedication

Dedicated to those who have suffered the agony
of war, the loss of loved ones, the confiscation
of ancestral property, and who now share the
deprivation of refugees, the anguish of nonentity,
the despair of fading hope, and the humiliation
of second-class minorities. To the dispossessed
Palestinian people this book is dedicated with
the hope that they will seek what Anis Shorrosh
has found: light amidst darkness, liberty in life,
and love that overcomes hate.

Foreword

What drives young revolutionaries to hijack airliners, plant bombs, and make daring raids across borders knowing in advance that they stand a good chance of being killed? Anis Shorrosh, the subject of this biography, knows that it is neither money, fame, nor love of a woman, but dedication to a cause. Anis Shorrosh understands this because his greatest desire once was to seek revenge. And his story, which is one of the most exciting I have ever heard, will help you understand the motives behind the Palestinian commandos who could possibly trigger a world war.

Anis is one of the few Christian Arab evangelists in the world. To my knowledge, he is the only Palestinian evangelist of renown living today. As a Palestinian, who was born in Jesus' hometown of Nazareth, he bears the one message that could heal the enmity between Arab and Jew. His message is credible, because he is living proof that Christ can turn bitter hatred to love.

I first met Anis in a seminary classroom. He was known for his infectious smile and amazing ability to learn. It was years later, however, that I really came to know this "man from Nazareth." After meeting him again at a convention and learning that he had recently come from Jerusalem, I invited him to speak to our church in Merritt Island, Florida, near Cape Kennedy. When Anis began to speak, it was only a few moments till that large crowd was caught up into a glorious spiritual excitement. There were tears and gales of laughter and many decisions for Christ.

Since then, I have heard him and watched him minister on many an occasion at home and abroad, and each time seems more refreshing than the last.

For my many friends who may not get to meet Anis in person, I could only wish that they will be able from the pages of this book to feel something of the heartbeat of "the Liberated Palestinian." He has found the answer which the diplomats need to know.

ADRIAN ROGERS
Pastor, Bellevue Baptist Church
Memphis, Tennessee

Preface

The Middle East. Hallowed. Controversial. Crisis plagued. Center of attention for world watchers from the adult Bible class at the corner church to the Security Council of the United Nations.

Want to start a quick argument? State an opinion about recent history in Bible lands. Or make a prediction about the future there.

No other area of the world holds such interest, especially to American evangelical Christians who pore over Bibles, flock to prophecy conferences, and buy millions of books that attempt to analyze the events and forecast the future.

There is no single accepted viewpoint on what has happened there and what will happen, though many evangelical Bible scholars hold that the birth and preservation of the modern state of Israel is a fulfillment of certain prophecies of Scripture.

This true story expounds the recent history of the Middle East conflicts from the viewpoint of one who lived it—a Palestinian Arab born and reared in Nazareth, the hometown of Jesus—one whose life later was transformed by this same Jesus.

The authors do not attempt to tell all that happened during this period. They simply relate the unusual workings of God in the life of Anis Shorrosh as they occurred in the swirl of wars and national passions that surrounded him.

This book, therefore, presents historical events as viewed by the one man who lived through them. It does not attempt to explain, interpret, justify, or condemn. It merely presents the experiences of Anis Shorrosh as he lived them.

It is a narrative that readers will not soon forget, a telling of a most remarkable conversion and life.

JAMES AND MARTI HEFLEY

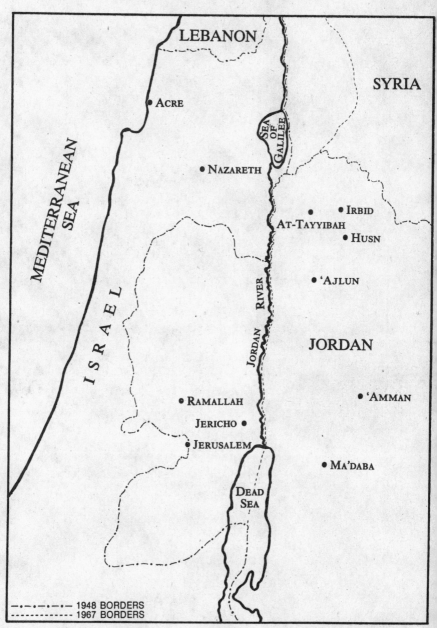

Palestinian locations for Anis Shorrosh's early life and later ministry.

1
THE CONFLICT

Anis Shorrosh trudged despondently up the hill toward his grand-parents' home on the outskirts of Nazareth. Above him sheeplike cumulus clouds drifted lazily across the blue Palestinian sky, giving no hint of the bloody conflicts that raged to the west.

Frowning under his mop of ebony hair, the 15-year-old youth kicked violently at any pebble that dared block his path. Surely his mother had devised this errand to send his scowling face from her presence. Did she expect him to be cheerful? The year 1948 was no time for a Palestinian lad to be happy, especially when his father had been taken away again.

"Anis!" an aging voice rang out. "Your appearance has brought joy into my day." The lines in the old woman's face creased into a delighted smile.

"A happy day to you, my grandmother," Anis answered respectfully. "My mother sent you this wool that remained from knitting Samuel a sweater."

"It was kind of you to bring it," she replied cheerily. But her good humor could not erase the look of discouragement Anis had worn since he had visited his father the week before.

"You've had a long, hot walk. Perhaps a drink from my well will cool you," she suggested. "I thought I might bake some *tabun* bread." The mention of the fragrant bread she baked in her outdoor oven brought a softening in Anis' eyes, and the faint hint of a smile. With this encouragement, she set to work.

He shuffled over to the vine-shaded well, took a long cool drink, and splashed some of the refreshing liquid on his face. Standing there on the crest of the hill, he could see the sleepy, sand-colored village of Nazareth stretched out in a crescent shape to his left. Except for the domed mosque that rose above the flat stone-roofed residences, the town had changed little since Jesus had walked the dusty streets nearly 2,000 years before.

He could hear his grandmother humming as she kneaded the dough. It was kind of her to try to lift his spirits, but what did any Shorrosh have to be glad about?

The family name had not always been Shorrosh. He was a member of the Christian Arab tribe known as Rihani, but when his bedouin forefathers had left their black tents of the desert to put down roots nearly 300 years earlier, the other members of the tribe began calling them *Shorrosh*—"the rooted ones." Young Anis Shorrosh was well rooted in Nazareth.

Impulsively, Anis decided to climb into the spreading branches of the huge old *kharoub* tree that shaded his grandparents' front yard. As he snuggled into the comforting branches of a favorite fork in the tree, he worried about what the future might bring to his people. He had been nicknamed A'baid, "the black one," because of his velvety black hair, but today the name was doubly appropriate because of his dark thoughts.

He gazed out across the verdant green Megiddo valley and rolling Galilean hills swelling with the growth of springtime. Could this land be taken from his people? They had lived here for generations. For centuries. And yet rumors abounded that all would soon be lost.

He thought of the old Bible woman, Em Kaleel, who lived up the hill from his house. How enthralled he and his friends had been by her stories of biblical heroes—David, Daniel, Joshua. But when she turned to prophecy and said that the Jews would one day rule again in Palestine, she would lose her audience. Crazy old woman. Or was she?

Until recently Anis had never felt the Jews to be a threat. Refugees from the European holocaust had been welcomed by most Palestinians. Half the population of Nazareth belonged to Christian Arab tribes, most of whom would agree with his mother who reasoned, "Why shouldn't they have an opportunity to live in peace?"

Anis had agreed with this philosophy, believing the Jews would be good citizens. Hadn't he heard stories of how earlier Jewish settlers had paid respectable sums for land along the coast and with irrigation had made the desert bloom like a rose?

But when word came that the United Nations was going to divide Palestine to provide a homeland for the Jews, Anis had felt resentful. What right did those foreigners have to give away land which the Palestinians had owned for so long? The Jews had been grossly mistreated by Hitler, but that didn't mean they should turn on the Palestinians. It just wasn't fair.

Yet there was no denying the massacre at Deir Yassin. Anis shuddered as he remembered, a cold chill crawling up his spine in spite of the warmth of the sun. Deir Yassin was a small village a few miles west of Jerusalem where Arabs and Jewish settlers had lived together in peace for many years. When warnings were given for those living in possible combat zones to move to safer villages until after the conflict was settled, no one left Deir Yassin. They had had no troubles there.

Then in April, despite the fact that the British mandate had not expired, Jewish troops had occupied the town. With the town secure, the soldiers withdrew, leaving members of the extremist Irgun and Stern groups to control the villagers. These terrorists then proceeded to butcher 254 Arab men, women, and children. The revolting atrocity was climaxed by throwing the mutilated bodies into a cistern and then parading the captured Arab women through the streets of Jerusalem. Crowds jeered at them and spit upon them with such vehemence that terror spread to the hearts of Arabs throughout the land. The trickle of evacuees became a torrent.

If there really is a God, how could He permit such things? Anis wondered. The question made him feel a little guilty, for he had been taught that it was wrong to question God. He had been born into a Christian tribe, had attended the Baptist mission church and school, and yet he had doubts. Was God really like what the American missionaries had told him?

God, they had said, was a heavenly Father. But what was a father really like? Most of what Anis knew about his father, his mother had told him. Some of his earliest memories were of his mother gathering Assad and Kamleh, his older brother and sister, himself, and baby Samuel around the flickering kerosene lamp before bedtime.

His mother was as great a storyteller as their ancestors who had woven the famous plots of the tales of the Arabian Nights. She would tell them stories from the Bible, and of magic, kings, and finding great treasures. And often, as they sat wide-eyed on their mats around the short-legged table, munching on watermelon seeds she had roasted for them, she would reminisce about Augustine Shorrosh.

"He was a good man, your father," she would say, and Assad, Kamleh, Anis, and Samuel would nod in agreement. People had always told them this was so. "Though, naturally, I did not meet him until after the marriage contract was made. I was very shy at that first meeting. I wanted him to like me, but I worried that he might think I was too small to be a strong wife.

"But the very first time I saw him—so tall and straight and handsome—I looked into his kind brown eyes, and he gave me one of his bright smiles. I knew this was a good man. He would be a good husband.

"He was a hard worker—a cobbler with nimble fingers that fashioned strong boots and sandals. And with the birth of a son he became known as 'Abu Assad,' the father of Assad, instead of Augustine, just as I was no longer Olga, but Em Assad, the mother of Assad. He was very proud of each of his children, and loved you very much.

"He built this strong stone house for us. He worked so hard to provide for us. Perhaps his dreams were a little too big, a two-story house with two large rooms in each, and a kitchen on the ground floor. When he ran out of money to finish, I gave him my gold dowry bracelets. I knew how important it was to him that we have a home."

The children were always properly impressed with this information, for they knew how important an Arab woman's dowry was. They had never heard of any other mother giving up her dowry for a home.

"Your father was not merely a member of a Christian tribe, he was a true believer," she would continue. "He was one of the first converts of the Baptist missionaries. And after our marriage he told me how only Jesus could forgive sins, so I too received Him as my Saviour and was baptized.

"But one day when he was on a train, he began handing out pamphlets to the passengers that told the Christian message. Some

Muslim fanatics who were also on that train became angry and turned on him.

" 'Dog!' 'Blasphemer!' 'Heretic!' they called him, forcing him to the back of the railroad car. One of them grabbed a long-handled hatchet from the wall, one that is used for emergencies, and came after him menacingly.

" 'Peace, my brothers. I meant no harm,' he told them. But they kept coming. His only hope was to jump from the moving train.

"He must have hit his head on rocks when he fell, for when he came staggering home he was bloody and whimpering in pain. He fell on his mat and lay there for days. I called the missionaries, but they could do nothing. They said he must have suffered brain damage.

"He just lay there, with glassy eyes, seeing nothing. Sometimes he would call out, reliving the scene on the train. It was very sad; I could not help him.

"Then he got worse. He would make noises like an animal. Throw things. Break or smash everything in sight. He was so big and strong that I was terrified. How could I protect you children? When he turned on me, I fled to the church seeking refuge. Leo Eddleman, the kind missionary from America, made arrangements for your father to be admitted to a hospital in Lebanon where he could be cared for. Now we can only live with hope that one day he might be well again."

Anis snorted sarcastically as he thought of that great hope that he had nurtured all his life. His mother had gone to work in the Baptist orphanage. "Until your father comes home," she had said. His uncles Daoud and Tamim had helped support their brother's children in accordance with Arab tradition, "until he returns." For so many years he had dreamed about that great day.

The sweet aroma of the *tabun* bread baking in his grandmother's oven wafted up through the branches to his perch high in the tree. But even that could not turn him from his tortured memories.

He had waited so long for his father's return, depending on his uncles for masculine influence as he grew. The boys all had male teachers in school, and that helped. Especially Dr. Eddleman. Anis remembered how hard he blew on his trombone—his face would get so red that he sometimes worried that the veins in his neck might pop.

It had been Leo Eddleman who rescued him the time he had

fallen on the playground during recess and cut a deep gash in his head. The missionary had carried his bloody form a mile up the hill to the British lady doctor who sewed up his wound. Yes, Dr. Eddleman had helped fill the gap left by his father.

When Assad turned 16 in 1945, he had taken a job on the oil pipeline in Jordan. This helped the family finances, for each month he dutifully sent home part of his pay, as was expected of young men in their culture. The $48 helped, but it also meant that at 12 Anis became the "man in the family." He took this responsibility seriously, and did odd jobs in Nazareth after school and during summer vacations. It was a hard life for an adolescent.

And then the telegram came. "AUGUSTINE SHORROSH IS NOW WELL STOP HE HAS BEEN RELEASED FROM THIS INSTITUTION STOP SHOULD ARRIVE IN TWO DAYS." Oh, joyous day! What a celebration they had. The whole clan had gathered for the feast in his father's honor.

They ate *mansaf,* roast lamb served on great mounds of rice and sprinkled with pine nuts and slivered almonds, topped with yogurt. His uncles shot guns in the air, announcing to the entire village the return of Augustine Shorrosh. There was laughing and shouting and singing.

Then his father returned to his cobbler's bench and they settled down to be a normal family. But all too soon it became apparent that Augustine was not really well. He was not violent, just forgetful; he would wander around in an absent-minded daze. Some said he was childish; others that he acted senile. Anis wasn't sure which, or if it made any difference; he just knew his father wasn't normal.

It soon became apparent that for his own safety he had to be put away somewhere so that he would be given adequate security. Because there were no facilities available in Palestine for the mentally ill, the sheriff made arrangements to commit him to the penitentiary in Acre. Anis felt ashamed to have his father in jail, but he was comforted by the thought that at least he would be safe there.

Now all those dear to him were gone. The missionaries had left because of the threat of war. His uncles had moved to Jordan. And his father was locked up in prison. Who could blame Anis for feeling bitter? It seemed his whole world was falling apart.

The trip to the penitentiary had been the final blow. When his mother decided to visit her husband last week, Anis insisted on accompanying her. But the experience at the ancient fortress in Acre had been horrifying. The dilapidated old Crusaders' fortress with its moat and ramparts was depressing in itself, but while waiting for his father they saw a British guard beating one of the inmates. Anis would never forget the sickening sound of the soldier's club splitting the prisoner's skull.

What kind of treatment was his father receiving? He seemed all right, but it was so difficult to communicate with him. Visiting hours were soon over and Anis had watched sorrowing as his father was led back into the dungeon. Would he ever see him again?

"Anis, Anis, come, eat while the *tabun* bread is still hot."

He looked down into his grandmother's kindly face, and with a sigh, climbed nimbly to the ground. He didn't really feel like eating, but he couldn't hurt her feelings. He felt certain she had prepared his favorite delicacy just to make him feel better.

He forced a smile when he saw she had laid out some sweet honey figs and white *lebani* cheese with the *tabun* bread. "*Shukran*," he thanked her sincerely, as he broke off a piece of the bread. The light in her dark eyes made him feel that perhaps she understood his bitterness and frustration. Impulsively, he reached out and gave her a warm embrace.

Encumbered with bread and fruit to be taken home for the others, Anis started the long trek home. Nearing the marketplace, he saw groups of men huddling together, talking excitedly. He stopped at the barber shop where he worked occasionally and asked what had happened.

The boisterous chatter and animated gestures of the group there ceased. They looked at one another silently, then away. A few shuffled their feet. Finally the barber cleared his throat and explained.

"Acre has fallen," he announced solemnly. "The last Arab city on the coast. And it wasn't even included in the territory given to the Jews."

"Acre!" Anis gasped, "but my father is in Acre."

"We know," the kindly barber nodded sympathetically.

"But what will become of him? Will he be killed?"

The barber shrugged and shook his head. Anis turned on his leather sandals and hurried down the street before the stinging in his eyes became uncontrollable. In his mind he could hear the old Bible woman crackling in an I-told-you-so voice, "The rebudding of the fig tree! The rebudding of the fig tree."

Augustine Shorrosh, Anis' father,
wedding portrait at age 25.

Olga (Em Assad) Shorrosh, Anis'
mother, wedding portrait at age 16.

The Nazareth Baptist Church, near the traditional Mary's Well on the main road to Cana, where the Shorrosh family worshiped.

Special group of singing boys at the Baptist Day School in Nazareth, 1940. Anis is front right (finger in mouth).

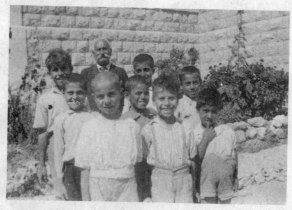

2
THE ATTACK

Since the middle of May rumors had intermingled with news bulletins spreading panic across the usually placid little town of Nazareth. With the British gone, there were no soldiers to protect the ancient village.

"Fallett hukum"—"no longer is there rule or order"—was an often heard phrase. The Palestinians had been ruled by foreign powers so long they had no idea how to bring order to the chaos that resulted from the British leaving. Now the Israelis were on the offensive.

As the summer wore on the advancing Jewish forces would broadcast their latest victories and announce which towns could expect them the following day. Driven by terror, many residents would pack what belongings they could carry and flee to the east. Thousands passed through Nazareth on their journey to safety.

In the schoolyard Anis and his young friends would discuss the happenings and rumors.

"The Jews don't really have a chance of taking over Palestine," Fowsi, Anis' cousin, declared confidently. "I don't understand why they couldn't just be content being allowed to live here. Why do they want to take over and run our country?"

"Just wait till the Arab countries get together," Fuad, Fowsi's brother, prophesied, "then they will be sorry they ever started this fight. Why, the Arabs outnumber them so we could beat them using just sticks and stones. We'll slaughter them."

"Yeah," agreed Anis, his black eyes shining. "Egypt and Saudi

23

Arabia will come from the south, Jordan and Iraq from the east, and Syria and Lebanon from the north. We'll push the invaders into the sea!"

"Yeah! Yeah!" the group of optimists gathered around shouted. "We'll push them into the sea!"

But outside the walls of the school yard the populace was far less confident.

Mail delivery had stopped and the only communication with the outside was from the radio and the distraught people fleeing through Nazareth. Each afternoon the Arab-controlled station in Jordan would broadcast personal messages from people anxious about their relatives in embattled Palestine. When the time came for the 15-minute daily broadcasts, all activity would cease in Nazareth while the people huddled around radios, hoping to hear from friends and loved ones.

"From Fuad Hassin to his relatives in Jaffa: 'We have arrived safely and all is well. Mother and Father, please try to join us.' "

"After a harrowing trip, Ahmed Ali Nasser from Safad is pleased to announce the birth of his firstborn in Jordan. He is to be named Muhammed."

"Habib Fawzi was separated from his family as they fled from Haifa. He can be contacted through the United Nations in Irbid, Jordan."

"The family of Ibn Saladin desires word of their loved ones in Acre. It has been weeks and we have heard nothing."

Anis sympathized with that family, for he had received no word from his father either. The only news that had come was that all the prisoners had been released from the old fortress prison before the fall of the city. Unless someone helped him, Anis doubted if his father could find his way back to Nazareth.

Tension and insecurity kept building in Nazareth. There was no army to protect them. Rumors persisted that the Syrians would be coming to their defense, but days and weeks had passed, and no help came.

While the Jews kept up their psychological warfare, more and more Palestinian Arabs passed through Nazareth seeking sanctuary. Many came on foot with only the clothes on their backs. Anis even spotted one man in his pajamas and thoughtlessly laughed.

"Just you wait," the thin-faced Arab prophesied. "When terror strikes your heart, you will not think it so funny."

"I'll not be scared away from my home," Anis vowed cockily. Just the same, he kept listening to the Israeli broadcasts.

The broadcasts would open with militant martial music that made Anis shiver. Then the announcer would speak in smooth Arabic.

"A happy evening everyone. This is the news. You have heard of the tremendous advances of the Israeli forces. We continue to be victorious in conquering pockets of resistance wherever we find them. We have the upper hand. We advise that you be prepared to surrender whenever the liberating troops appear.

"Be assured that we wish to kill no one. We only want control of the land that is ours by historic right and by approval of the United Nations. We urge you to surrender peacefully. But if blood must come, it will come. We are fully capable of meeting all resistance, and if necessary we will fight and defeat the forces of all Arab nations. We will be victorious!

"Today we successfully entered the village of Shefar'am and tomorrow we press on to Nazareth . . ."

Anis blinked. His mouth went dry. His muscles tightened. "Nazareth!" He glanced at his mother's ashen face. Her eyes were round with fear, and yet there was no sign of tears.

"We must pray," she said simply.

"Pray!" Anis snorted rebelliously. "I'll pray for a gun. A machine gun! And I'll kill any Jew who tries to take our home."

"No! Didn't you hear what that man just said? We must not resist."

Many of their neighbors packed what they could and fled. The sparsely traveled road that ran through the town was crowded with terror-stricken Palestinians who felt they must leave till after the battle. At the junction of the two roads leading into Nazareth that formed a Y at Mary's well, there was even a traffic jam. An unheard of event in that ancient town.

In their little farm home on the outskirts of the town, Anis' grandparents discussed their plight. Should they leave as some of their children had already done?

"We're too old to run," the grandmother sighed. "Too old to leave this land we've farmed so long. It would be best to die here."

Her silver-haired husband nodded in agreement. *"Inshallah,"* he whispered. "If God wills it."

It was a long fear-filled night. There was little sleeping and much praying. "If only the Syrians would come to help us," was the thought in many hearts.

The sun rose hot and clear the next morning. The tension was so great it seemed the whole city was holding its breath. From the northwest a cloud of dust was rising. Many eyes watched from the flat rooftops as the cloud came nearer. Then as the roar of powerful motors was faintly heard, a cry went up. "Syrians! See the markings. Syrian tanks! The Syrians have come to save us!"

The shout rang from street to street. "The Syrians have come to help us!" The people who had remained ran cheering from their houses to hail their Arab protectors. There was loud clapping of hands, and much hugging and kissing as tensions relaxed and relief spread through the town.

A great crowd assembled along the highway that entered Nazareth from the northwest. As the tanks rumbled closer the cheers rang all the louder. The green, white, and black Syrian emblems that glistened on the tanks never looked more beautiful.

Inexplicably, unbelievably, the tanks opened fire. The crowd gasped, momentarily too stunned to react. Then a sharp eye saw that the sloppily painted-on Syrian emblems were hiding Stars of David. "They're Jews!" a terror-stricken voice rang out. "It's a trick!"

In blind, unreasoning panic the people ran as the tanks fired volley after volley over their heads. Into the nearby olive groves. To the desert. The barren wilderness. Pushing. Shoving. Children screaming for their parents seeking a place to hide. Some were still in their nightclothes. Many struck out for the Lebanese border, never turning back.

Anis had remained with his family in the courtyard of their home. When they heard the shooting, he and his brother Samuel climbed on top of the high wall that ran along the side of their house and strained to see what was happening.

The car of a neighbor, chauffeur to the police chief, careened around a corner, and screeched to a halt. They saw the policeman dash into his house, pulling off his uniform as he ran.

If he is afraid, the Jews must really be here, Anis thought.

The sounds of shooting came nearer. "Mother, the Jews are coming!" Anis screamed. "We must find a hiding place."

"The cave!" Em Assad cried as she and her daughter Kamleh ran from the house to join the boys. Hurriedly, the four dashed up the hill to the yard of a neighbor who had promised them refuge in a storage cave shaded by citrus trees. As the Shorroshes moved toward the back of the damp, gloomy cavern, they recognized the voices of other neighbors cowering in the darkness.

A shell hit nearby and the earth shook as dirt fell on them from the ceiling. A young girl cried out in fright, and to her great embarrassment, vomited.

"Why are they bombing us?" Anis demanded, shaking a defiant fist at the unseen enemy. "They must know there are no soldiers in Nazareth."

"They are probably just trying to scare us," an elderly man replied softly. "We must remain calm, or we will only make the children more frightened."

"How do you know?" the girl who had vomited shrieked. "Maybe they will make of Nazareth another Deir Yassin. Oh, why didn't we run when we had the chance? We're trapped in here like animals. We'll never get out. Never." Her voice rose higher and higher as she became more and more hysterical. Her father hurried to her side, placed a comforting arm around her as she wept uncontrollably.

Anis looked at his mother and sister. They were obviously frightened, but he was quite proud of the way they were conducting themselves.

Rifle shots and occasional machine gun bursts continued as the afternoon wore on. The crunching sound of running footsteps came nearby a few times, and everyone held his breath, but there was no attempt to enter the cave.

"I wonder how your grandparents are," Em Assad whispered into the darkness. "They are so exposed up on that hill. They have no cave."

"Also Suhail and his parents," Anis added, thinking of his cousin with whom he played often. They lived farther up the same hill from the Shorrosh home.

"Yes, our cousin goes to work so early. I hope Em Suhail is not alone with her son," Em Assad sympathized. Then she stopped and reviewed her own position. "But, it's best, I'm sorry to say, it is best that your father is not with us. He wouldn't understand, and the noise would frighten him so."

"I'm hungry," Samuel complained after a while. "Why didn't we bring something to eat?"

"Yes, we should have thought of that," Anis agreed. "I'll go for food."

"No, my son," Em Assad cried out, "you'll be killed."

"I'll be careful," Anis called back, and he dashed out before anyone could stop him. He crouched down by the garden wall in their host's backyard. He crept along this wall, crossing the yard. He paused, glanced around, and then made a dash for the side of the house. A burst of machine gun fire followed him. He wasn't certain if it had been aimed at him or not, but he didn't wait to investigate.

Pressing his lean young body against the side of the house, he glided along, making the smallest possible target. When he reached the road he hesitated. There was no possibility of crossing without exposing himself. He waited until a lull in the firing, took a deep breath, and ran like a gazelle.

He reached the other side safely, slid down beside the stone wall near the steps leading down into his own yard, and let out his breath slowly. He felt more secure with a wall to hide behind, but just then a bullet whistled past his ear. He scrambled madly down the steps, dashed across the yard, and into the safety of his home.

He quickly crossed the cement block floor of the main room, climbed the five steps into the kitchen and began rummaging for food. He put fruit, olives, bread, and cheese into a bag, thought about the others in the cave, and picked up a basket of figs. Their cupboards weren't exactly overstocked, but they would share what they had.

He paused in the doorway of his home, looking down into the valley. Puffs of smoke made the sounds he had heard all day seem more real. What were they shooting at? Stealthily he climbed the high fence to get a better look. He spotted the distorted bodies of three men lying in the rutted narrow street below his home. He swallowed hard, then decided he had better hurry back to the cave before his mother became worried.

Climbing the hill, he was facing the direction of the shots which had so narrowly missed him before. He preferred it that way. He proceeded cautiously, but deliberately, pausing only at the road to check for snipers. Then in one long dash, he crossed the street, ran past the house, across the yard, and into the cave where he received a hero's welcome.

"Oh, thank God you are safe!" Em Assad exclaimed. The tears she had been holding back so bravely all day now began flowing freely. She took her son's face in her hands, and kissed him enthusiastically on both cheeks, stopped to blow her nose, then kissed both cheeks again.

"It's all right, Mother, I'm fine," he assured her. "And I brought food."

The shooting continued about them as night fell. With the coolness of evening Anis noticed his mother shivering, "I should have brought blankets," he thought aloud.

"No!" Em Assad declared emphatically. "I'm not cold."

"But we will be before the night is over," he predicted. "If I wait until dark it will be easy to slip back to the house."

Despite his mother's protests, he left as soon as darkness shrouded the beleaguered town. This trip was less eventful and he was glad for the excuse to leave the stuffy cave and get a breath of fresh air. With no sanitary facilities, and so many people crowded together, the cave was becoming more and more unpleasant.

Warmed by the sweaters and blankets Anis brought from the house, the Shorroshes huddled together in the dark, wet cave, fearful of what the new day might bring. There was little sleep for anyone.

It was after dawn before all the guns became silent. But instead of comfort, the silence brought more fear. What was happening? Was it another trick to draw the people from their hiding places? They spent another two or three apprehensive hours listening—listening for some clue as to what would happen next.

Finally Anis and a few men ventured forth to scout out the city. No one shot at them, so they checked for damage to the homes. The silence was deafening. Nazareth seemed a ghost town. Were they the only ones in town left alive? The eerie quiet made Anis' flesh crawl.

They could spot no danger, in fact no damage at all, so they called for the women and children to come out into the sunshine. Em Assad and her youngsters hurried down the hill and into their home.

All over Nazareth similar scenes were taking place as the suspicious inhabitants emerged slowly from their hiding places. As families regathered, some loved ones were missed.

Shortly after the Shorroshes had returned to their home, a

knock came at the door. Apprehensively, Em Assad looked through the curtain of the large window to the right of the door—it was a Jewish soldier! A sergeant. Glancing into the courtyard she saw three more soldiers, all with submachine guns. The next knock was louder, more insistent. "Open up in there!" the sergeant called in perfect Arabic.

"Wh-what do you want?" Em Assad asked nervously wiping her palms with her handkerchief.

"We are just making a house-to-house search for weapons. Open the door."

Resolutely she opened the door and stepped out of the house, pulling the door partially closed behind her. Anis and Samuel were both frightened, but their curiosity was even greater, and they stuck their heads out of the doorway to see what was going on. Kamleh held back in the house, hesitant to be seen by the soldiers.

"*As salam 'alaikoom*," the sergeant greeted them politely in Arabic.

" '*Alaikoom salam*," Em Assad replied, trying to keep her voice from trembling.

"Do you have any weapons?"

"No, nothing. We have no man here. Just myself and my three children."

"Are you Christians?" the soldier inquired, evidently knowing that half of Nazareth's Arabs were of that faith.

"Yes, we are Christians."

"Well, we know good Christians don't lie. If you will give me your word you have no weapons, we will not search your house. Just tell us truthfully, do you have weapons of any kind?"

"No. No weapons."

The soldiers looked at one another hesitantly. Anis began to perspire, terrified they might ask him, for, unknown to his mother, he had buried a bayonet in a pile of sand near the house. Finally the sergeant jerked his head toward the neighbor's house and said to the soldiers standing behind him, "C'mon, let's get this over with."

Em Assad hurried back into the house where she clung to her children in relief. "Thank God!" she murmured over and over. "Thank God for His protection."

Soon another knock came. This time it was a somber Palestinian friend. He stood twisting as if it were painful to speak. Finally he said, "I bring sad tidings, Em Assad. Your first cousin Abu Suhail has been killed."

"Oh, no," she gasped and covered her face in shock. Behind her Kamleh began to cry softly. Anis' and Samuel's faces were frozen.

Then recovering, Em Assad asked quietly, "How . . . when . . . what happened?"

"Yesterday when the attack came, he was hurrying home to be with his family when he was sprayed with machine-gun bullets. The funeral is this afternoon; his wife has asked for you to come, if you feel it is safe. She doesn't want the children. His body— well, he was nearly cut in two by the bullets; it would be better if they did not see.

"And if I may give a word of advice, I don't think I would allow a beautiful, young, marriageable daughter out on the streets," he added gently, nodding toward Kamleh.

"You are right, of course," Em Assad agreed determinedly. "Her brothers will protect her while I attend the funeral."

"Mother, do you think it is safe for you to go?" Kamleh protested.

"Em Suhail needs all the comfort she can get now. They won't bother a group of middle-aged women going to a funeral," she assured her daughter. Turning to the friend she pulled herself to her full 4'10" and declared, "I'll be ready to join the funeral procession as it passes by on the way to the church."

Later, Kamleh, Anis, and Samuel gathered at the window to watch their mother leave. Anis was seething inside. Abu Suhail had been such a good, gentle man. He didn't deserve to die in such a brutal manner. And poor Em Suhail was now a widow. Hadn't she known enough tragedy? Wasn't her firstborn son, her only child, a deaf mute? How would she carry on? Who would look after her? It seemed so unfair.

The three young people stayed huddled close together while their mother was gone. It was amazing how much strength such a tiny woman as she could have; they didn't realize just why, but with her gone they felt even more frightened.

The days that followed were difficult. Fear continued to grip the people. When would the Arabs ever come to help? Had they been abandoned? And if Arab soldiers did come to deliver them, would they be caught in the crossfire between the two armies?

With the town under martial law, the women could go to the shops and wells only at certain times. The food supply in the town was dwindling rapidly, for no trucks were allowed in from the countryside. The only goods being brought into the town were contraband, and these were smuggled in at great risk, for there were many encounters with the border guards.

With no mail allowed from Jordan, funds from Assad and their uncles stopped. Fortunately it was summer, and the Shorroshes, like most families in Nazareth, had a small vegetable garden and a few fruit trees. But not all these were ready for harvest, and the growling of stomachs made frayed nerves even more touchy.

Em Assad tried to keep her children inside the house, but Anis rebelled. He couldn't stand being cooped up so much. Besides, he felt it was his responsibility to try to find work so some money would be coming into the house. He went by the tailor's shop where he sometimes earned a little doing odd jobs, and was distressed to find Jewish soldiers looking through the wares. Most shocking were the female soldiers wearing shorts! He turned his head in embarrassment; he had never seen women in such scanty attire. But then his pride was hurt, for one of them dared order him back to his home. At 15 he considered himself a man and found the command deeply humiliating.

Every afternoon the family clustered around the radio to hear the messages broadcast from Jordan. Some were heartbreaking, and the listeners never knew when the announcer might say next that one of their loved ones was dead. But they had to listen. They had to know.

"The family of Miraim Masoud is desperate for news of their beloved son Moain. They have heard no news since he left for Jordan six weeks ago."

"We sorrowfully announce the death of George Salameh, his wife Anisee, and their infant son. All were killed attempting to flee occupied Palestine."

Sometimes the tragic announcements would get to the broadcaster and he would break down and cry. Sitting beside their radio, the Shorroshes would share his emotions.

About six weeks after the fall of Nazareth a message finally came for them: "To the family of Augustine Shorrosh. Assad Shorrosh begs you to leave home and join him in Irbid, Jordan till the situation is more stable. He has no way to send you money, and cannot provide for you unless you come to him."

Samuel jumped up excitedly on hearing from his brother. "Let's go—now!"

Kamleh sat wringing her hands. "But so many have been killed trying to leave. It's too dangerous," she wailed.

Anis had remained the calmest of the three. He turned to Em Assad and asked, "Should we go to Assad, Mother, and stay until life is better here?"

Em Assad looked up at her son who was already taller than she. "I don't know. How could we get there? The busses are not running, and we have no money anyway. It is too far to walk. I just don't know about this idea. We will have to pray about it."

3

THE EXODUS

A gentle tap, tap, tap on the front door reverberated in the silence of the night. Cautiously Em Assad opened the door a crack to see who would be coming after curfew. The flickering light from the kerosene lamp reflected on the face of a stranger wearing a black and white checked *keffiya*.

"As salam 'alaikoom," the soft-spoken traditional greeting came. "I bring word from your son Assad."

" *'Alaikoom salam,"* Em Assad answered breathlessly. "Come in, Friend. Come in. How is my son? Does he know we are all right?"

"Your son is very concerned for your safety. He begs you to come to Jordan where he can protect you and provide for you. It is impossible to get money across the border. I managed to bring certain articles across with me, but not cash. It is too dangerous."

Then bowing courteously and touching his hand to his heart and head, the nameless stranger slipped into the night.

"We must pray," the perplexed mother declared. "We must pray that if God wants us to go, He will provide the money we need. And a permit that will allow us to travel safely."

The next morning before the hot summer sun had reached its full heat, Em Assad set out for the courthouse, where the Israeli soldiers had established their military headquarters. The huge stone structure looked more imposing than ever as she neared the building where the blue and white Israeli flag now flew. She paused outside the main entrance, made certain her blouse was tucked into her skirt securely, adjusted her shawl, and clutching her purse tightly entered the long, dim hall.

She paused before a wide desk in the main corridor, which seemed the obvious place to ask for information.

"I would like to apply for a permit to visit my son in Jordan," she explained to the blue-eyed soldier with a fresh crew cut.

"A permit?" the incredulous soldier echoed. "A permit! Ha! Ahhhaaa, ha, ha," he roared, leaning far back in his swivel chair. "You need no permit, woman. Go," he exploded with a wide gesture of his arm. His amusement turned to a snarl as he added, "And good riddance!"

Shaken by the vehemence with which that admonition had been spoken, Em Assad hurried out. The bright light of the sun momentarily blocked her sight, but not her vision; she was now determined to get her children away from these invaders. As her eyes began to focus again, she decided to investigate what modes of transportation were available.

After asking discreet questions in a number of the shops in the *suq* (marketplace), she found a camel driver who would at least discuss the possibility of taking the family to Jordan.

"The safest thing to do is pack enough belongings so that you look as if you are moving to another town," he said. "Those who carry only small satchels are usually jumped on first, for the looters think all their valuables are in that one bag. If you have some bed rolls and a couple of pieces of furniture on the camel's back, you look less enticing to those unscrupulous jackals who prey upon the misfortune of others."

"I thank you for your advice. Now if God wills us to leave, He will provide the money for the trip. I thank you for your willingness to risk crossing the border with us."

"My only son was killed during the takeover of our town," he replied sadly. "Since then my life has not seemed so valuable. I know your circumstances; I will be glad to help any woman with the sole responsibility of three children."

"*Shukran,*" she repeated her thanks. "*B-khatirkum.*"

"*Ma-salami; fi aman illah.*"

Em Assad was greeted by three excited children. "Mother, people were here asking to rent our house for a while. They will be back to see you," Anis reported. "Perhaps this means God wants us to go."

The grateful woman smiled. "God has provided. We can rent to them for three months. Surely things will be more settled by then and we can return."

When the people interested in renting the house returned, Em Assad made arrangements with them and they paid the rent money. Then the Shorroshes began packing. They stuffed clothes into cotton sacks, rolled four pillows and four cotton mattresses into tight bundles, adding four quilts and a few pots and pans to the stack along with a few food staples, and rolled out Em Assad's massive handcarved wardrobe, her husband's wedding gift to her.

"If we take any furniture, it will be that," she declared when Anis tried to convince her it was too large and heavy. "Your father gave it to me. If I leave it and the renters should break the mirrors, I would never forgive myself. It can be taken apart and tied to the camels' backs."

Anis knew from the set of her jaw that logic would be useless. It took three men to tie the pieces of the prized possession on one of the three camels the driver brought to their home. And the camel complained louder than the men. It groaned, grumbled, wheezed, and griped until Kamleh felt sorry for it.

"Poor thing. Its back will surely be broken," she sympathized.

"Pay no attention to that old grumbler," the owner chuckled. "Camels are neurotic by nature, and that one particularly so. He's carried much heavier loads with ease."

The little caravan started out that mid-August afternoon. The driver led, riding on a donkey, and the three camels followed, carrying the Shorroshes and their belongings. The driver had removed the traditional bells from the camels' necks. He didn't want to attract attention.

Anis felt his bedouin blood tingling with excitement, for he had never ridden a camel before. As they left Nazareth on the groaning beasts and followed the camel trails through the valleys, the journey seemed like high adventure. The plan was to travel during the daylight hours to the driver's home in a tiny village nearer the border. There they would sleep a while before taking the more dangerous part of the journey, and make the actual crossover in the dark.

Something about the jostling, ungainly gait of the camels appealed to Anis. The sun was hot on his back, but there was a cool breeze on his face, so it was not too uncomfortable. As the camels started around a hill that would block Nazareth from sight, he twisted in his saddle for a last look at the picturesque village spread over the hillsides in the distance. A pang of loneliness struck his heart and he had the strange sensation that he might never see his homeland again. "This is silly," he told himself. "We'll only be gone a few months."

They were out in the open country when an Israeli plane flew over them. They watched as it slowly banked to circle back over them. As it came straight at them, dropping closer all the time, their driver shouted, "To the walls. They might shoot!"

They scrambled off the animals and ran to the nearest stone wall that had been built by some farmer years before to prevent erosion.

Pressing himself as tightly as he could against the rocks, Anis tried to make himself as small a target as possible. He could feel the blood throbbing through the veins of his temples, his heart was beating so hard. Each second he expected to hear the chatter of bullets. This was surely to be the end of his life.

But the pilot did not fire. After a few leisurely passes over the terrified travelers he apparently decided they were harmless and flew away. Anis breathed a deep sigh of relief and wet his parched lips, but he never regained the carefree exuberance he had felt when they first began the trip.

"It is good we have the children and the furniture," the driver told Em Assad. "They must have presumed we were just moving. We will soon reach my village and there we will spend the night."

They moved on. Once they passed through a desert area littered with burned-out tanks and jeeps punctured by bullets. The sight of the debris of war was unnerving.

When the driver finally pointed to his village in a small valley below, they felt safer. Even the camels seemed anxious for rest and stepped up their awkward pace as they started the descent. Anticipation of the stop made Anis forget for the moment the stiffness caused from bouncing on his camel's back.

At last they reached the camel driver's home. The camels obediently dropped to their knees, allowing the riders to slide off. The driver escorted them into a dingy square room where they would sleep for a few hours on the dirt floor. Then he returned to feed the wheezing animals.

They were putting down their personal belongings when the

driver suddenly returned. Anxiety was written across his leathery face. "If you know how to pray, pray," he said. "A jeep is coming."

Anis pulled back a burlap curtain and peered through the window. The jeep that had stopped outside carried four Israeli soldiers and machine guns mounted front and back. Had the plane radioed the soldiers to check on them?

He heard his mother praying. "Dear God, protect us. Please help us get to safety. Help us find a place where we need not live in constant fear. You are our only hope, Lord. Please make them turn around and leave us alone."

To Anis' great astonishment, just as his mother had requested, the jeep turned around and took off in the direction from which it had come. *Maybe God really does answer prayer,* he thought.

After a frugal meal the family rolled out their mats on the floor of the room that served as communal sleeping quarters for the camel driver, his family, and several other travelers. Em Assad and Kamleh were very nervous lying in a place with strange men and slept little. When the night was darkest their driver called softly.

"Come, we must begin again. Back to the camels."

Anis was awake and alert instantly. He shook his sleeping younger brother. "Samuel, come on, Samuel," he whispered.

They quietly rolled up their bedding and carried it out to the unenthusiastic animals. The camels complained more than usual, evidently venting their displeasure at having their slumber disturbed.

The passengers were even more uncomfortable on this leg of their journey, for they were sore before they started. Em Assad had raw places on her legs where constant chafing had rubbed open sores. They had plodded through the darkness for less than an hour when her camel swayed unexpectedly, and she fell to the ground with a section of her precious wardrobe tumbling after her. Anis dismounted, hurried to his mother's rescue, and dusted her off while she tried to regain her composure. The travelers strapped the piece of furniture more securely on the camel's back and cajoled the distrusting woman back into the saddle.

At the driver's insistence the camel unfolded its long limbs and moaning balefully, rose to its feet. The little caravan resumed its nocturnal journey.

They had made little more progress when Em Assad's camel

made another unexpected dip, hurtling her to the ground. She jumped to her feet and indignantly shook her fist at the beast. "He did that on purpose!" she wailed. "I know it. He did that on purpose!"

The camel snorted indifferently, causing her to burst into tears of futility. "It just doesn't like me. I refuse to get back on it!"

"You can do it," her children encouraged her.

"We must get to the border before dawn," the camel driver warned anxiously. "He just wanted to roll in the dust he found in this soft spot. He'll be all right now."

Despite all reassurances she remained adamant. Finally the driver relented and permitted her to ride the rest of the way on the back of his more gentle donkey.

Finally, at 3 A.M., they reached the bank of the Jordan River. The crossover would be the most dangerous part of the trip. But the risk had to be taken. On the far side was safety and protection in Jordan.

Em Assad got back on a camel and urged the animal into the dark swirling waters. Behind her came Kamleh and Samuel, with Anis following on the third camel. As the water lapped around Kamleh's feet, she thought she was being swept downstream by the current and screamed. Reassuring voices called from both sides of the river. Behind her, Anis rode more confidently, surprised at the narrowness of the stream.

"Welcome, *Lajieen.*" The tall Arab who greeted them and assisted them down wore a warm smile. *"Lajieen?"* Anis questioned. The word was unfamiliar to him.

"You'll learn what it means all too soon," the man replied cryptically. Soon Em Assad had struck a bargain with the man to drive them into Irbid in his small, black pickup truck.

The fare represented the last of the rent money, but it was a relief to leave the camels behind. Best of all was the feeling of security that prevailed. They were safe here.

The first streaks of dawn were lighting the horizon as they entered the Jordanian town of Irbid. Anis was surprized at its small size. There were just a few little hole-in-the-wall shops on the main street.

Passing through the main section of town, they turned right and followed a twisting street until the driver deposited them at the home of Uncle Tamim.

After a joyous reunion with their relatives, the weary travelers enjoyed some peaceful sleep. There were no bombs, machine guns, or snipers' bullets to be heard. In Irbid there was not even a curfew.

When Anis woke late that afternoon he thought it was the next day; he had become completely disoriented by the trip and the unsettling schedule. Uncle Tamim and Em Assad had gone to look for a room to rent, since the relatives' apartment was already crowded with cousins.

Anis was a little set back to learn that Uncle Tamim had reverted to using the ancient tribal name of Rihani, since this was a large and well-known clan in Jordan. *Not me,* thought Anis. *I am not a nomad without a home. I'll keep the name Shorrosh; I like being "rooted."*

His mother returned to say she had found a small room for them nearby. Assad was working at an oil field called H-4, and would not be able to see them till his day off, but had left money for them to rent the room. The white limestone house with the flat cement roof did not look particularly inviting to Anis. It was not nearly so nice as their cut stone house in Nazareth. The four of them would have to sleep in the one room, his mother would cook with charcoal on the clay stove outside, and there was an outhouse. Not the most luxurious accommodations, but it was only temporary.

When the huge handcarved oak wardrobe was assembled, it looked strangely elegant in the modest surroundings. The three giant mirrors reflected the four sleeping mats that had been laid on the floor.

A few days later Assad arrived. There was much hugging and kissing and giving of thanks. Nearly 20, Assad looked tall and handsome with the new mustache 15-year-old Anis envied.

Assad said he was the assistant manager of Spinney's supermarket at H-4, the pumping station near the border of Iraq some 150 miles east of Irbid, but business was bad. "The only industry there is the Iraq Petroleum Company, but they have stopped pumping oil to Haifa now that the Jews are in control there. They are keeping a skeleton crew till things get back to normal, but that means there are few customers for my store. Back when things were booming I could have found work for Anis, but not now."

This news was discouraging for Anis, who was finding too much time with nothing to do most boring. He had worked every summer for the past five or six years and felt at odds with the unaccustomed idleness. Perhaps Uncle Tamim could use him in his little jewelry shop.

While they were together, Assad borrowed a car to show them some of the Jordanian countryside. The rocky terrain suffered by comparison with the fertile fields of Galilee. The sandy wadis and rocky fields cried out for moisture. Anis found the landscape depressing, but most dismaying of all were the tent cities erected for the Palestinian refugees.

From a distance the camp looked like a brown blur on the high ground north of Irbid. As they drew nearer, Anis could see long lines of khaki-colored tents, so small that two would fit in one room of his home in Nazareth. They were staked close together in long, monotonous rows. Each one contained a family of *lajieen*—refugees; a word he now understood.

The *lajieen* were from towns all over Palestine, where they had once lived happily before their land had been taken by the Jews. Now they had no homeland, no citizenship. They were a people without a country. They belonged nowhere.

But we are not like them, Anis assured himself. *We will be visiting here with our relatives only a few months. Then we will return home to Nazareth. We will never be* lajieen.

Assad drove them back to Irbid, where Uncle Tamim agreed to let Anis work in his shop. Anis and his cousin Ghassan swept out the shop, ran errands, and occasionally waited on customers; when time permitted, the artisan their uncle employed tried to teach them the jewelry-making art. The skillful craftsman whose back was bowed by long years of bending over his work would patiently demonstrate the tricks of his trade to the disinterested cousins.

Anis found this apprenticeship difficult. The strain of working on such tiny bits and pieces was hard on his eyes. He would blow through the ten-inch-long copper tube forcing air across the fire so that it would melt the metal while he shaped it with his fingers. His hands were soon full of blisters and burns from trying to forge tiny links in a silver chain. He despaired of ever learning to make delicate earrings and brooches. Besides, he hated being cooped up 12 hours a day in the small shop.

The main enjoyment in the job came when his uncle left the two cousins in charge of the shop. Then they would take down the heavy antique swords that lined the upper part of the high-ceilinged room and play Zorro, clanging the valuable swords against one another until the little shop vibrated with the noise. They were gleefully involved in such a duel one day when Uncle Tamim returned unexpectedly. That ended Anis' career as a goldsmith. At least for a while.

There was another delicate family affair that needed to be settled. It was Naifi, Tamim's wife, who brought it up first. Kamleh was of marriageable age. Why had no wedding been arranged?

"The situation in Nazareth has been very unsettled this past year," Em Assad explained. "But when we return I'll have to see about finding her a suitable husband."

"But we have many fine young Christian men here. Surely a match could be found for such an attractive young lady. She is tall and strong, and no doubt could bear many children."

"But when I return to Nazareth, I would have to leave my only daughter behind. No, I think it is best to wait until we return."

Fall came and the beginning of the school year. All the cousins returned to their classrooms, but there was no place for the refugees. "Let's go home, Mother," Anis begged. "I'll work hard on my studies, truly I will. I'm not happy here. I want to go to school. How will I ever make anything of myself with only seven grades of schooling?"

"I understand, Anis," Em Assad sympathized. "But it is too dangerous. No one is being allowed back across the border."

"But what about our house? The rent period will soon be over."

"I left our good friend and neighbor George Khaleel in charge of the house. He will collect the rent and if need be find new renters. Our property is safe."

But the "temporary" arrangement dragged on and on. Soon the weather began to cool. Assad's contribution and the small pittance Anis had earned in Uncle Tamim's shop were not enough for food. Reluctantly, Em Assad took Samuel, Kamleh, and Anis to the United Nations office in Irbid and applied for a ration card. There were 12 numbers around the edge of the card, representing the 12 months. Each month when their allotment of food—flour, peas, butter, rice, beans, and a few other staples—was given, a hole was punched through a number. As the weather became colder, warm clothing and blankets were distributed.

When Anis first looked at their card a strange choking sensation gripped him. It was just a 3"x5" card with the words UNITED NATIONS RELIEF AND WORK AGENCY printed on one side and their names on the other, but it represented their only proof of existence. Now that the Jews controlled their land, they were a people without citizenship, passports, or a homeland.

Even more fearful was the thought that this card might mean he was one of the *lajieen*. When would he be allowed to return to his home?

4

THE EXILE

Em Assad shook some chick-pea seeds into the lid of a large tin can, added some water, and then set the lid on the window sill of their crowded room. She was carrying out the Arab tradition of having something green growing to welcome the new year. It would soon be Christmas and the fast growing chick-peas would sprout in time.

The joy the Shorroshes felt when they first arrived in the safety of Jordan had slowly tarnished. The weeks dragged by with no sign that it would be safe to return. With the money Assad gave them and what little Em Assad could make doing needlework, they managed to scrape by, but the future looked bleak. There was no way to collect the rent money from their home in Nazareth.

Anis was particularly despondent over the school situation. He had always been a good student and wanted to continue his education, but this was impossible. Occasionally he would go with the tall, lumbering English missionary and translate for him. Anis had learned a little English at school, and liked to demonstrate his knowledge, since there were very few people in the city who knew any English at all.

The tall Britisher, Douglas Howell, and his diminutive wife were with the Brethren Church in Irbid, and held services in their home. Anis was more interested in learning English from them than in acquiring Bible knowledge. He enjoyed riding around town in their car, and he was particularly enamored of the British ceremonial tea each afternoon at four. The beautiful bone china Mrs. Howell would place just so, and the dainty way she poured impressed him as much as the sweets that were served with the hot tea.

The few occasions when he accompanied the Howells soothed his troubled spirit. If he had found a good job, perhaps he wouldn't have been so depressed. But with so many refugees— over 630,000 by this time—pouring into the tiny, underdeveloped country, the employment situation was drastic all over Jordan.

Listening to news broadcasts had become a form of masochism. It seemed as if the whole world for some unknown reason had turned its back on the Palestinians. Peaceful peasants who had spent generations doing nothing more exciting than tilling their soil, trying to eke out an existence, loving and taking great joy in their children were now outcasts. Families which had been so close-knit, extending to cousins of cousins until it sometimes seemed whole villages were related, were now torn asunder sometimes waiting months to hear of one another's whereabouts.

And all too often when news did come it was tragic, as the report from Jerusalem telling of the death of a young cousin. Subhi had been a handsome young boxer, the only child of his parents. A life snuffed out before maturity seemed doubly sad.

There was one bit of encouraging news that came over the radio to brighten the Christmas season a bit:

"We are happy to report the passage by the General Assembly of the United Nations of Resolution 194 (III), which offers hope to those who have been exiled from their homes in Palestine. Paragraph 11 of this resolution reads as follows: 'Resolved that the refugees wishing to return to their homes and live at peace with their neighbors would be permitted to do so at the earliest practicable date, and that compensation should be paid for the property of those choosing not to return and for loss of or damage to property which, under the principles of international law or in equity, should be made good by the governments or authorities responsible.' "

"That means we can go home soon!" Anis shouted gleefully. His enthusiasm cheered his mother, brother, and sister, who had not been listening as attentively as he.

"Do you think we might be in Nazareth for Christmas?" Samuel asked.

"That would be a little soon, Son," his more pragmatic mother replied. "We will wait and see how well the resolution is enforced."

"But will we perhaps be home in time for the new school term?" Anis asked hopefully.

"We can only hope and pray," she answered noncommittally, but the smile on her lips and the sparkle in her dark eyes encouraged Anis, Samuel, and Kamleh to believe they could return soon.

They were waiting for more assurance that it would be safe to return when a woman friend from Nazareth, now living in one of the *lajieen* tent cities, stopped by. Em Assad made Em Moain comfortable on the mats which the family stacked during the day to form a sort of couch.

They talked for a while about the prospects of returning home, then the visitor squirmed uncomfortably and looked away. "I am so sorry to hear about your husband," she said.

Em Assad sat bolt upright. "My husband? What have you heard? We have heard nothing since the fall of Acre."

The distress in her voice alerted the children who had not been paying much attention to the women's chatter.

"You didn't know that he was dead?" the visitor asked incredulously.

"No, no. How did my Augustine die? I must know," Em Assad begged, tears coursing down her cheeks.

Anis' face whitened.

"I really don't know all the details, Em Assad. I just heard that he had been released with the others before the fall of Acre. There was no one to help or protect him, and he set out toward Nazareth. He evidently found a family of refugees who were traveling to our town and accompanied them. They arrived the same day the tanks came.

"When the battle ended late the next day, the family saw his body lying in the road. He must have been killed early in the battle. They knew his name, but did not know whom to notify, and were afraid to stay in Nazareth any longer. They continued their flight into Jordan. I just happened to meet the wife in the camp one day as we were standing in line to get water from the faucet. She told me the story when I mentioned I was from Nazareth."

"But where is he buried?" Anis asked in torment.

"I don't know. Unclaimed bodies are usually buried by the authorities. I'm sorry I don't know anymore. I didn't even think to ask the family's name. There are so many people in the camp it would be nearly impossible to find them again."

"I wish I could thank them for being kind to my Augustine," Em Assad murmured bravely. She sat staring into nothingness for a few moments. "And I thank you for bringing me this word. It is bitter news, and yet somehow I had felt for sometime that he must be dead, or we would have heard from him. It is better to know than to wonder endlessly."

She saw her friend to the door. They embraced in parting, and Em Assad returned to her one small room and her three children. Together they mourned the loss of their beloved husband and father.

"We should be thankful for the assurance that your father was a true believer, and that we will be united again someday in heaven. Now he is with his Lord, and he is well again. Well and strong and really alive for the first time in years," she continued, thinking of him as he had been before his fall from the moving train.

The very words that brought comfort to the widow stirred rebellion in Anis' heart. *The Jews killed my father!* The thought whirled round and round in his brain. *First the Muslim fanatics nearly killed him, and left him half a man; then the Jews finished him off. It isn't fair! God, if there is a God, hear me! I say it isn't fair!*

There was little reason for joy that Christmas. They were sojourners in a foreign land. Their father was dead. And their cousin Subhi. And Abu Suhail. The year 1948 had been indescribably sad for them.

"Yet we have much to be thankful for," Em Assad insisted. "We are cramped in this one small room, but at least we are not living in one of those horrible tent cities as so many of our countrymen are. I have four strong, healthy children. And we have safely survived a war. We have relatives here who care for us. And a church where we can pray and worship the Lord." But her optimism did little to heal the bitterness and hatred that kept growing in Anis.

With the new year, 1949, came reports of armistice agreements signed between Israel and the various Arab states. These were not peace settlements, but more a series of stalemates, each of which contained the statement: "The Armistice Demarcation lines should not be considered as the permanent boundary between Israel and her neighbors." In practical terms to the Shorroshes it meant they would not be going home for a while longer.

Em Assad decided that since they would have to stay in Jordan for the immediate future, they should find better lodgings. After days of diligent searching they found a two-room apartment in a nicer house. Their rooms were off a shaded courtyard studded with palms. There was a nice large front room and a cozy, small kitchen. They shared the outhouse with their landlord's family and one other family. It was a much more pleasant residence than the adobelike hovel they had stayed in for the past six months.

Anis got a job helping in a tiny shop in the local market, but because few had money to buy, business was slow. He earned only 25¢ for a 12-hour day, but it was better than nothing. He would have preferred a job where he had to work harder, for the time would pass more quickly, or else one where he could learn a trade. He would stick this out for a while.

The family continued attending the Brethren services. One Sunday the English missionary preached on confession of sin and forgiveness. Anis, now a grown-up 16, smiled to himself, thinking he had outsmarted God on that score some years before. As a child he had heard a similar sermon and decided he just wouldn't tell God about any of his sins. Then God would never know, and could not hold him accountable. Though he was now in his later adolescence, he still held the comforting delusion that God didn't know about any of his sins, for he had never confessed them. And he certainly wasn't about to start.

But there was another message that really bothered him. The British missionary said Christians should forgive their enemies! Anis slouched in his chair and scowled. *That's easy for him to say,* he thought, indignantly shooting a fierce look at this lanky man he used to think understood him. *Would he still say that if the Jews had killed his father! Forgive? I would die for the opportunity to avenge my father's death. If I could help rid Nazareth of the Jews that infest it like a swarm of locusts I would . . .*

And he continued brooding, planning vengeance instead of listening to the sermon.

Spring came and the end of the rainy season. Nazareth was so beautiful this time of year. The grandparents' farm would be budding with new life. But the green hills of Galilee seemed so far away. And Anis was only one of a million Palestinian *lajieen,* though he still refused to call his family that.

A May 12 news broadcast reported that Israel and the Arab nations had signed a "Protocol" agreement in Lausanne, Switzerland. A map attached to the agreement showed the old boundaries which Israel had violated. For a few days they had new hope; then it was announced that after being accepted as a member of the United Nations, Israel had unilaterally revoked the Lausanne document.

Anis gave up his shop job to assist an electrician. Perhaps he could now learn a worthwhile trade. However when he saw how the man was cheating customers, he quit in disgust.

He next worked as a common laborer—anything to keep busy.

The months crawled by. Each time Em Assad turned a new leaf on the calendar, Anis would think, perhaps, before another month is gone we will be able to go home. He spent much of his time daydreaming.

He remembered when electricity had first come to Nazareth. Having never seen an electric bulb before, he stared at the light in his home for hours, seemingly hypnotized by its continual glow. What magic, light without burning. But electricity really hadn't changed the sleepy little town that much. Everybody still went to bed when the sun went down. The elders couldn't seem to change.

And he remembered Mary's well. How often had he cooled his head and lips there after a long hot walk, or after playing a strenuous game in the school yard across the street. Tradition said this was the spot where the angel had appeared to Mary, foretelling the birth of Jesus, but Anis had never been particularly impressed. It was just something he had always known.

Had Joseph's carpenter shop really been right down the street from where Anis' father cobbled shoes? Anis had never really cared; he had been more impressed with stories of his father. Anyway, Jesus lived in a Nazareth now covered by the streets and buildings of the present town. Having shared the same hometown had never made Jesus seem any more real to Anis; if at all, it only made Jesus seem more human, less divine.

Anis wondered if they had *falafel* sandwiches back in Jesus' day. Thoughts of a delectable *falafel* from the little stand on the main street of Nazareth made Anis suddenly hungry. He could just see the man making one, taking the round double-layered Arab bread and slicing across the top, then as it opened naturally, filling it with the little fried patties made of peas and bean's and mixed seasonings, then adding some pickles. Mmmmmmmmm.

When Anis wasn't daydreaming he would read. Paperbacks, magazines, novels, comics, anything he could beg or buy. Occasionally he would find a book written in English and he would struggle to decipher the foreign language. Once in a while as a special treat he and Samuel would get to see a movie. Their favorite shows were Arabic-dubbed versions of Tarzan. But most days passed routinely.

Then one day late in the fall of 1949 a distinguished family group appeared in the courtyard. Em Assad took one look and motioned Kamleh into the kitchen. After the traditional greetings had been politely exchanged and introductions had been made all around, the spokesman of the group explained their visit. "We have come in behalf of my brother Naji Sahawneh and would like to approach your family in a noble and honorable way. My brother desires your daughter's hand in marriage.

"Our family is Christian and enjoys a good reputation in our community. Naji is a sergeant in the Jordanian armed forces. A fine, upright, decent young man. He could not give your daughter a palace but could provide for her in a worthy manner."

Em Assad's brain was whirling, trying to take in the full intent of this unexpected proposal. Kamleh was of marriageable age and they had postponed finding her a husband longer than intended. Still Em Assad would have to meet the boy first and ask the opinion of Tamim and Daoud. She gave Anis a questioning look. Anis raised his dark eyebrows expressively and rolled his eyes. Samuel seemed to be trying to keep from exploding into giggles. In the kitchen Kamleh, the object of all the discussion, had been listening through the door. Now she began drawing water, for in the Arabic culture if the girl's family was interested in a proposal and wished further discussion it was customary to offer the visitors coffee. She would have the brew ready if her mother wanted it.

In the living room the relative with the most "face," that is, influence or importance, continued to extoll Naji's virtues. "A kind, gentle man not given to great fits of anger. Very respectful toward his parents . . ."

"We feel very honored at your interest," Em Assad finally

commented. "But since we don't know the young man we will need time to think it over. For now may I offer you some coffee?" she asked significantly.

She waited anxiously for the reply. A refusal would mean they were no longer interested. The delegation exchanged glances and nodded agreement. "We would be very happy to have some coffee," the spokesman smiled. Em Assad hurried into the kitchen. She would have to serve it herself since according to custom they would not be allowed to see Kamleh on this first visit. To her delight, Kamleh already had the coffee brewing.

During the three weeks before the next scheduled meeting, the prospect of Kamleh's marriage was the primary topic of discussion among all the Shorrosh relatives. Everyone had an opinion and no one felt too shy to express it. Assad made a trip in from H-4 and went to Husn to investigate the Sahawneh family. He came back with a glowing report. From all indications it seemed to be a propitious match.

The Sahawneh family had presumably been conducting their investigation before making the proposal. Anis thought they might have seen his sister in church. At the time a Palestinian girl was held in high esteem by Jordanians. Palestinians, especially Christian girls, were usually better educated. Few Jordanian girls could read or write.

When the family returned, Naji accompanied them, bearing baskets of luscious fruit, sweet pastries, and candy—gifts for his hoped-for bride.

Kamleh ran into the kitchen when she heard voices in the courtyard. This time custom permitted her to serve the coffee. While the water heated she peeked through a crack in the door.

What an impressive sight the soldier made in his khaki uniform and red *keffiya* headdress with fancy handmade tassels. Kamleh also noticed how polite he was to Em Assad, and how gentle as he seated his own mother.

When she entered to serve the coffee and cakes, Kamleh hardly dared to breathe. She wore a new dress, pale green to set off her clear olive complexion. She was so anxious for their approval.

As she extended the tray to Naji, she glanced shyly but directly into his eyes. He flashed a wide grin revealing even rows of glistening white teeth. Flushed with embarrassment, she lowered her dark widely spaced eyes demurely, and hurried on to the next guest. Naji was enchanted. The rosy glow the embarrassment had brought to her cheeks made Kamleh all the more beautiful. Naji was not only content to set a date for their engagement, he was quite eager.

It was decided that the formal engagement ceremony would be held in Uncle Tamim's home, since it was much larger than the Shorroshes' little apartment and could better contain all the relatives from both families. The intervening month was busy, especially for the groom. He ordered material both for his bride's wedding dress and trousseau and new outfits for all her family, and in addition bought shoes and accessories. Most important, he made a trip to the goldsmith to purchase the rings and bracelets that would serve as his wife's dowry—an Arab woman's most precious possession.

Meanwhile, Em Assad and her women relatives were busy sewing. Uncle Tamim's wife, Naifi, was reputed to be the best seamstress in Irbid and Em Assad was quite skilled herself. Together, they made a team that would have been the envy of a Paris couturier.

Anis and Samuel had little else to do but watch the proceedings. As bolt after bolt of cloth was delivered, Anis realized why Arab men usually did not marry until in their late 20s or early 30s. "It takes them that long to save enough money to afford a wife!" he told Samuel.

The engagement party was a great occasion. A Greek Orthodox priest came from the groom's hometown, Husn, to perform the binding ceremony. Naji presented the dowry to Kamleh on a huge brass platter: six solid gold bracelets for her left arm, three gold rings, and a wide gold band for her right arm. She blushed and giggled and said everything was beautiful while the relatives oohed and ahed in the background. From this time on the young couple could see one another, talk, and become acquainted, but never be alone until after the final marriage vows were sealed.

It was now Naji's responsibility to prepare for the marriage ceremony and to find living quarters for after the wedding. Since he was in the army and would be unable to spend every night at home with his bride, it was decided that Em Assad and the boys should move to Husn to be near her and protect her when duty called him away.

Naji found a duplex-type house on top of a ridge overlooking the village. There would be two rooms for Em Assad and her sons and two for the newlyweds. The house even had indoor plumbing—a cement floored 4'x4' room with a hole in the middle.

It all seemed so exciting and romantic. Naji rented a bus to bring all his bride's relatives to the wedding service in the large Greek Orthodox church in Husn. A caravan of cars trailed behind the bus, with the passengers all singing and shouting at the tops of their lungs. Anis sang a favorite song for such an occasion: "Step on it, driver, we've got a bride in here."

After the solemn ceremony came the gala reception. When the singing and celebrating were over, each guest was given a token remembrance, a cut glass container filled with different kinds of candy and bearing the names Shorrosh-Sahawneh. As the newly-weds were about to leave, Em Assad noticed her new son-in-law look down into the smiling eyes of his bride. The contentment they shared in that glance caused tears to rise in her own eyes. At least one good thing had come from their exile in Jordan.

5

THE CONFRONTATION

Anis leaned against one of the three huge oaks that shaded his new home and watched resentfully as Samuel started off to school. He knew he should be happy for his younger brother, but he couldn't help feeling envious that there were only seven grades in the school.

After a few minutes he shuffled idly down to the pond where several of his peers were skipping stones on the water. They were a disgruntled lot, boys maturing into young manhood with no purpose in life and little hope for the future. Anis, nearing 17, had managed to grow a mustache. This, combined with the perpetual scowl he wore, made him the most menacing looking of the group.

When the sun became too hot for comfort, they retreated to some shade trees and plotted how they might recapture their homeland from the Jews. Their bitterness bubbled to the surface like hot lava in a crater as they concocted imaginary schemes for wreaking vengeance on the enemy. It was an excercise in futility, for they knew their schemes were impossible. They had no arms, no training, no military organization to join. But still they dreamed.

When Anis grew bored with the empty braggadocio, he returned home, flopped on his mat, and plunged into the newest paperback murder mystery Assad had brought on a recent visit.

Anis loved whodunits—the more blood, gore, and violence the better. The hate and bitterness that seethed within him seemed to feed on tales of brutality.

Sunday came and his mother, as usual, insisted he accompany the family to their church in Husn. Anis disliked the diminutive missionary-pastor named Victor Dudsworth. He found him ugly, unattractive, repulsive, and irritating, though he grudgingly admitted that this little man knew more about the Bible than anyone he had ever encountered.

Anis decided that *if* he were really interested, and *if* he really wanted to know the Bible, this was the man he would choose as his teacher. Then after learning everything the missionary knew he would memorize more Scripture than anyone in the world. For if he decided to do something, he would try to do it to the best of his ability.

But this was all imagination, for he felt no thirst for Bible knowledge. What he really wanted was a white dress shirt. Assad had given him a tie, a nice, bright blue, American-made tie, the first he had ever owned. But he had no shirt with which to wear it. He did have a white sport shirt, so he experimented with different methods of manipulating the collar so he could show off his splendid new tie. If he had to go to church, he might as well look his very best.

Finally he managed to insert two of his mother's straight pins in the flaps of the collar to hold them right. He really looked fine, but had to hold his head straight and rigid or the pins jabbed into his neck. With his head held high, he strutted off to the services much like a male peacock. Sitting stiffly in church, Anis glanced out of the corners of his eyes to see where the young girls were. He was not only interested in looking them over, but wanted to see if they had noticed him. Two shy smiles from across the aisle, and a fluttering of eyelashes to his right made him feel even more pleased with himself.

Then the preacher stood and read the sermon text: "His eyes are upon the ways of man, and He seeth all his goings. There is no darkness, nor shadow of death, where the workers of iniquity may hide themselves. . . . *He knoweth their works*" (Job 34:21-22, 25).

These last four words stunned the cocky young Palestinian. *He knows my works!* reeled through his brain. *He knows my works. Why, of course He knows. How stupid I have been to think that if I didn't confess my sins God would not know of them.*

The realization caused him to slink down into his seat. Two

sharp jabs from the pins brought him back to attention. "And God not only knows your works," the preacher was saying, "He knows your very thoughts, the intents of your heart. Listen to First Chronicles 28:9: 'The Lord searcheth all hearts, and understandeth all the imaginations of the thoughts.' "

Anis almost moaned aloud as the impact of these words hit him. He dropped his head in despair and the pain from the pins brought tears to his eyes. He wasn't sure which hurt worse, the pins or the guilt that pierced his heart. The rest of the sermon was blanked out by the blanket of doom that gripped him as he realized the enormity of his condemnation.

At the sound of the last amen, he dashed home and jerked off the tie that now seemed offensive and threw it across the room. He glowered at his reflection in one of the mirrors on his mother's wardrobe. "You are vain," he berated himself. "Vain and ugly and stupid. Why do you try to fool yourself that you are anything else? Trying to convince yourself that you are handsome when you are homely and full of pimples! Why not at least be honest enough to admit you are a sinful, loathsome creature, so full of hate that it erupts physically. You don't deserve to live."

Em Assad walked in just then and noticed the tie tossed carelessly aside. "Anis, is something wrong?" she asked, for he was usually neat and orderly. Instead of answering her innocent question, he pushed past her and ran off to be alone.

The next week he avoided everyone, preferring to spend his time alone hunting. He would sneak up on a little bird and shoot it with his 9 mm pellet gun, then pick it up and pull off its head. He had been taught to do this to a wounded bird to put it out of its misery, but he did it now for pure enjoyment. Twisting the head and pulling so he could feel the snap in the tiny neck bones fulfilled some deep longing, and the blood that spurted out brought a release he didn't really understand. He killed hundreds of the helpless winged creatures this way.

The next Sunday he refused to go to church. It was the first time he had openly rebelled against his mother, but he had decided to quit being a hypocrite. He couldn't fool God; why try to deceive others?

Instead he walked the five miles into Irbid and saw the movie "Forever Amber." He enjoyed the racy American movie so much he sat through it a second time. The next day he wrote in his diary, "The individual who enters movie houses forgets his pains and his problems for a very short time."

A few days later he returned from hunting to find his mother greatly upset. "What happened?" Anis demanded. Wringing her hands, the distraught woman explained that a man, one of their distant cousins, had come by to visit while she was at home alone and made romantic overtures.

Anis exploded. "How dare he? I'll get him for this."

"No, no, Son. Don't get into trouble. It's all right. He's gone now. Please, please, don't get in a fight."

But Anis was thinking of a revenge far more drastic than a mere fist fight. Scenes from old murder mysteries floated around in his head. A "hunting accident," he decided, would be the proper action.

A few days later he borrowed a powerful Remington rifle from a friend, and then invited the "cousin" to accompany him and Naji on a hunting expedition. "The fields are full of birds," Anis told him, not mentioning the insult to his mother. The cousin took the bait, and the three started hiking toward the wilderness surrounding the little village. Anis was quiet and scowling as they walked along, but that was nothing unusual. The others had no inkling of what lurked in his mind.

When they were out of view of the village, Anis raised his gun and aimed it directly at the cousin's head. Through the gunsights he saw the blood drain from the man's face and a look of horror fill his eyes. "You have insulted my mother!" Anis yelled. "It is my duty to avenge her; I am going to blast your head off."

All the hate that had been building up in him the past years seemed to concentrate in his trigger finger as he slowly began to squeeze. At the last instant Naji knocked the gun away, causing the shot to go awry.

"You young fool!" Naji screamed. "Give me that." He wrested the gun from Anis and emptied the magazine and Anis' pockets of shells. Then he slammed the gun to the ground and stomped back to town. Anis could do no great harm now.

Anis, however, scrambled to his feet blind with rage. Thwarted in his plan to shoot the offender, he took after him using the gun as a club. Swinging with all the force he could muster, he delivered a blow that sent the man crashing to the stony ground.

"Take this, and this, and this," Anis snarled as he kept beating the man with the gun. Screaming and pleading for mercy, the man curled into a whimpering ball, seeking frantically to ward off the blows. Not until the poison was out of his system did Anis stalk away feeling he had brought the affair to a satisfactory conclusion.

The naiveté of that thought was revealed when two policemen came for Anis a few hours later. The cousin was pressing charges against him. Naji accompanied him to the police station and spoke on his behalf.

"He is a young man with a great sense of duty," he told the officer in charge. "He felt it his responsibility as the eldest son living at home to protect his mother's honor."

"But we can't just let him get away with attempted murder," the official replied with a wag of his pointed beard.

"He is a Rihani; why not let the tribal clan judge him?" Naji suggested.

Since the tribal law often superseded governmental laws in Jordan, the man agreed, and Anis was brought before the men of the clan. They ordered him to apologize.

"I apologize to the tribe for bringing dishonor to the highly respected name of Rihani, but I will not apologize to the cur who insulted my mother," he replied stubbornly.

"Then you must leave our town, never to live here again," they decreed.

So, after a turbulent year, the Shorroshes and the Sahawnehs left Husn in disgrace.

Back in Irbid Anis found his reputation had preceded him. No one wanted to give him a job. Finally his Uncle Tamim relented and gave him another chance at being a goldsmith. He wasn't really needed, and was treated like an indentured servant, but his uncle felt at least he was keeping the rebellious youth off the streets.

Anis hated the job. It had no future, and only paid 25¢ a day for 12 hours, seven days a week. He and his cousin Ghassan had outgrown Zorro by this time and no longer spent idle time in play. Now they discussed the news and wove intricate stratagems to overthrow the Jews. They were particularly infuriated over the plight of the wretched refugees who had now been living in the depressing tent cities for nearly three years. There was talk of building more substantial dwellings, but the *lajieen* refused to consider this. They feared it would just make their condition permanent.

The one enjoyment that Anis had at this time was flirting with the girls who came into the shop to buy jewelry. Though Arab custom strictly forbade any physical contact with a girl until after marriage, he would fondle the hands of the young customers as he helped them try on a ring or bracelet. The touch of soft skin and the blush that resulted gave him a thrill. The very danger of being caught making such advances made the flirtations all the more daring, and much more fun. Girls were not even allowed in the same school classes with boys, nor were they allowed in movie theaters when men were present.

The moment came when he was slipping a ring on a delicate finger and he looked up with a sensuous grin to meet a bold pair of black eyes returning his suggestive look. He was so flustered; he didn't know how to react. Later he daydreamed of what might have been. And he thought about what he would do the next time that girl came into the shop.

Then he realized his hypocrisy: *Why, I tried to kill a man for this very thing. I am no better than my despicable cousin. And God knows all I have been thinking and planning. What a wretched, miserable beast I am!*

On top of this revelation of self-deception came the most distressing news of all. Uncle Daoud's sister-in-law had been one of the few allowed to cross the border for the Christmas holidays. She reported that the Israelis had confiscated the Shorrosh home. "They consider it an 'abandoned property,' " she explained sadly.

"Abandoned!" Anis exploded. "We would go home tomorrow, if they would not shoot us the moment we crossed the border."

"My dowry," Em Assad wailed. "That house is my dowry." She dissolved into bitter tears. She had been brave through as much tragedy as she could take. This was too much. Her tears flowed for days. When her eyes were finally dry once again, Anis could see in them the hopelessness he had seen in other *lajieen*.

The realization that they were never to return to their home threw Anis into a deep depression. Life seemed so hopeless. Uncle Daoud arranged for him to work as a waiter out in the desert for the oil company that was putting in a huge new pipe line. The job was for a few months only, but Anis hoped to follow them on into Iraq, and so applied for a Jordanian passport. The passport was granted "under the third article," which meant that he was a refugee from Palestine.

Anis found the desert interesting, especially the black volcanic rocks that were scattered about. It was the first time in his life he could see for as far as his eyes would permit. He had always lived among hills before.

When the construction was completed, the crew decided not to take any Jordanians with them into Iraq. So Anis was left behind. Totally despondent, he returned to Irbid. Even this slight hope had evaporated. Now he had no father, no country, no home, no education, no job, no future. There seemed no reason to continue living. In total despair he contemplated suicide.

If I could only get a machine gun, he thought dejectedly. *If I had a machine gun I would get back across the border somehow and I'd slaughter just as many Jews as I could before they killed me. My life has been totally meaningless; at least that way my death would have some value.*

He knew it was impossible. He even lacked the means or skills for ending his barren, meaningless life. He turned and ran outside . . . down the dusty street . . . across rocky fields . . . running . . . running . . . with no destination . . . no purpose. Except to die.

Stumbling along over the rocky terrain, he thought of his forefather Ishmael who had been cast out into a wilderness similar to this. It seemed so unfair. If God was just, why did it seem He loved Jews more than Arabs? Why should he be punished for being Ishmael's descendant, when he had done no more wrong than his illustrious ancestor.

Darkness was falling and he stubbed the big toe of one of his open-sandaled feet on a sharp rock. All signs of civilization were far behind him by now and he started searching for a smooth place to spend the night. He cleared some stones from a flat depression, and using a rock for his pillow, lay down. As the night turned to indigo and then to velvety blackness, he wondered how the desert would kill him. Starvation? Dehydration? Wild animals? Or perhaps a poisonous viper would end it all quickly.

He was extremely uncomfortable as he lay there watching the stars appear. The rocky soil felt like a bed of nails, the chill of the desert night caused him to shiver, and the cries of distant night animals were unnerving. As his eyes swept across the starry heavens the thought came over and over, *God knows my sins. God knows my sins. God knows my sins.*

How ignorant he had been to believe he could fool God, as he had often fooled others. He remembered his childhood, how people always seemed to think he was a good little boy. If only they knew. Why once he even tried to wreck a train!

He had been visiting relatives who lived near a railroad track. All the adults were in the house talking and he had wandered outside by himself. He began thinking how exciting it would be to see a train wreck. Then he began piling stones on the tracks, the biggest he could manage. He was working diligently on this project, and had made quite an imposing pile when he felt the tracks beginning to vibrate. A train was coming.

Heart pounding, he had run and hid behind the stone wall that surrounded his relatives' house, but at an angle so he could witness the destruction of the locomotive. Only then did he stop to consider that people were on that train—people who might be killed. Instead of remorse, he had felt only fear that he might be punished for causing the wreck.

The train came nearer and nearer. It was too late to stop it now. The blood ran through his veins in time with the clickety, clickety, clickety sound of the approaching train. As it drew near to the pile of rocks on the track, he let out a piercing scream and put his hands over his ears as he watched in terror. The huge engine hit the rocks and crushed the sandstone to gravel. It continued on its way unimpeded and Anis had shuddered with relief.

What stupidity, Anis thought as he twisted down into the desert sand seeking what warmth was left from the day's sun. *I might have killed dozens of people just for a thrill. What a wretched child I was—thinking only of myself.*

The idea of self-centeredness brought back another memory. The annual Easter egg hunt they used to have at the Baptist mission school. The first year he had been allowed to participate, he had run about like a rabbit, gathering more eggs and candies than anyone else. But when all the goodies were placed in a large basket and divided equally among the children, he felt he was being unjustly treated. He had found the most!

He brooded about that for a whole year, and the next Easter had prepared a hiding place near the fence that ran between the school and church. He hid most of the treats he found, turning in just enough to keep the teachers from becoming suspicious. Later that evening he hurried back down the hillside, across the street and into the school yard to see if his treasure was still there. He pulled back the vines, and there lay the colored eggs and shiny covered candies. Covertly he sneaked them home to another cache; then he had enjoyed them one by one for several days.

And I never even thought about sharing, Anis thought remorsefully. *It didn't bother me a bit that because I had so much other children would be deprived. I was as selfish about the Easter treats as I was with marbles.*

Fights over marbles had earned him the nickname "Abu Barjes," the name of the notorious murderer who also had jet black hair. And he had been proud of the name. Proud of being a bully who always won the most marbles—if not fairly, then by force.

He rolled over on the hard desert floor and pounded his fists in the dirt. "What a mean, selfish creature I am," he moaned aloud. "Always thinking of myself. Never worrying about how I was hurting or taking advantage of others."

He thought of Em Raja, the tender-hearted neighbor woman who had saved him from many a well-deserved switching. He used to howl, "Help! Help! Someone please save this poor innocent child," whenever he saw his mother breaking off a pomegranate branch. "She is going to beat me! Please somebody help!" he would call, and Em Raja would hurry from her house calling, "Mercy, Em Assad, have mercy on him. He's just a little boy, and so sweet. You'll be good now, won't you, Anis?" And he would nod his head vigorously. "You see, Em Assad, there is no need to whip him."

"How many times did she come to my defense?" Anis wondered aloud. "And then in the dark of evening I would sneak into her orchard and steal her fruit! How loathsome. Not only a thief, but to steal from a friend!" He was filled with remorse and shame.

"And now?" a Voice from the night seemed to ask.

"And now I hate," he answered truthfully. All the teachings of Jesus seemed to burst from his memory. Since earliest childhood he had been taught that love was the fulfillment of the commandments, and yet he was so overwhelmed by the hatred that was eating at his insides that he felt nauseated.

"I hate the Arabs because they attacked my father. I hate the British because they exploited us and then abandoned us. I hate the Jews for taking our homeland. I hate the Jordanians and

Syrians for not coming to help us. I hate . . . I hate . . . I even hate myself. Oh, God, let me die!"

And there on the very plains where Jacob had fought with an angel many centuries before, Anis wrestled with his conscience.

6

THE TRANSFORMATION

By dawn Anis was exhausted mentally and physically. He felt sore, stiff, and hungry, but he had lost none of his resolve. He was still determined to end his life.

As the sun rose to its zenith, he realized what a horrible death the desert bequeathes to those unfortunates who fall victim to its powers. With no tree or bush to offer shade, the sun beat on him. The heat and the arid dryness sucked his body moisture and symptoms of dehydration soon beset him. His mouth was parched, his lips split, and his temperature mounted.

By afternoon he no longer had enough energy to stumble around, and he just sat waiting for the end to come. He hadn't realized how long it would take, or how miserable he would feel. His vision began to blur and his tongue seemed too large for his mouth. He longed for a drop of cool water. *This must be how the rich man felt in the parable Jesus told,* he thought. *No wonder he begged for Lazarus to bring him just a drop of water. Water. Such a precious thing, water.*

By the time the flaming orange ball began descending, he was becoming incoherent. He would alternately laugh aloud, mocking himself, and cry torrents of tears. In this half-dazed condition, he began thinking, *This is what hell must be like.* Incongruently a chill ran up his spine. He hadn't really considered hell, but he knew that if such a place existed he would be a ripe candidate.

He could not surrender to the desert and take a chance on hell. At least not now. Reluctantly, painfully, he dragged his aching

bones upright and started stumbling toward home. He had failed in what he had set out to do. His conscience and the fear of judgment and hell had defeated him. He had always hated admitting defeat on any score, but this was the ultimate failure. He couldn't even be successful at suicide.

It was long past dark when he fell into his mother's arms. "Anis, I'm so glad you're home," she sobbed. "I was so worried. Why did you go off without telling anyone where you were going? I died a thousand deaths not knowing. Sometimes I thought you might have tried to cross the border in pursuit of vengeance. Oh, Anis! Anis! My son!"

"Please give me food and water," he croaked, collapsing onto a mat by the low kitchen table.

Em Assad brought water and some cabbage rolls drenched in yogurt. Despite his hunger Anis ate little before dropping into an exhausted sleep on the cement floor of the kitchen.

The next day was Easter Sunday. Anis refused to leave the house. He spent the entire day lying on his mat and reading his mother's Bible. For three days he read and read stories he had heard all his life. Somehow they seemed different now. For the first time he began to think that the Bible might be Supreme Truth, not just a collection of old traditions. He came to the Sermon on the Mount, which he had memorized years before, and stopped at: "Seek ye first the kingdom of God, and His righteousness; and all these things shall be added unto you" (Matt. 6:33). He closed the Bible and lay staring at the ceiling for a long while.

The battle flared again in his soul. Could this promise be believed? Could God "add" to his miserable life all that he had been seeking—peace, purpose, hope, meaning? Could God lift the guilt that was knifing his heart?

He would have to seek God *first*. That was what Jesus demanded—first place. His life would no longer be his own. He would not be free to lust, to scheme, to hate for any reason.

He could fight no longer. In true contrition he knelt beside his mat and prayed, "God, if You are real, You will keep Your word. I am holding You to this verse. From this day on I will seek Your kingdom, Your way, and I will depend on You to take care of me. I have made such a mess of my life, but I know You can forgive me and put me on the right road. Please begin by giving me a job."

Since early childhood Anis had been taught that forgiveness of sin and a new birth were available to those who put their trust in Jesus. He had believed intellectually that Christ had died for his sins, but had never turned in repentance and faith to call on Christ as his Lord. Now that he truly believed, he was flooded with a peace and joy he had never imagined.

He rose from his knees and walked into the kitchen where Em Assad was at work. "I'm hungry," he said quietly.

His mother smiled. "Well, finally your appetite has returned."

Anis smiled at her.

"What has happened, Son? You seem different."

"Oh, I'll tell you later," he grinned and plunged into the food she had set before him.

With his stomach content, he went outside for a walk. The world looked different that April 1951 day. The birds sang sweeter. "A happy afternoon to you," he called to an old man passing by.

He walked boldly, confident in the future, though he was a youth of 18 without a job in a country where unemployment was pushing 40 percent.

That evening he went gladly to prayer services in the Howells' home and shared with the believers his new joy. His shining face convinced everyone that he had indeed experienced the new birth which Jesus said all must have to enter the kingdom of heaven.

Afterward he floated home, ecstatic in his new faith, singing all the way. Too happy to go to bed, he dropped in next door and stayed up past midnight discussing the miracle of salvation with his brother-in-law, Naji.

At home again, he knelt beside his mat and thanked God once more for the new life. "Let me be happy and rejoicing," he asked. "And please provide a job."

The answer came faster than Anis ever imagined. Just three days later Assad came from the pumping station at H-4 with exciting news. "I've been promoted to manager of the supermarket," he exclaimed, pounding Anis on the back. "And I can choose my new assistant. Who do you think that will be?"

Anis' eyes rounded with wonder, his mouth slowly spreading into a wide grin. "Me—an assistant manager for Spinney's?"

"Oh, you'll have to go for an interview," Assad explained. "But that's just a formality, since you'll be the only one applying for the job. It pays $60 a month, in case you're interested."

Anis beamed. "Sixty! I've never earned more than eight." Then as he came back to earth, tears welled in his eyes as he realized God had provided far beyond what he had dared hope.

"Well, praise the Lord!" Anis shouted, hugging his older brother and kissing both his cheeks. "Praise the Lord!" And he grabbed his mother and danced her around the room. "God really answers prayer!"

After filling out the job application, Anis went to Amman and was baptized by a Baptist missionary just as his mother and father had been many years before at Nazareth.

A few days later he was driven in a company car to the British-owned supermarket chain store at H-4. As assistant manager, he would be trained to keep books, take telephone orders, and be groomed for a managerial opening in the future. With Spinney stores all over the world, prospects for advancement seemed unlimited.

Besides the salary, which was at least four times what the average unskilled laborer earned, he was given a clean, air-conditioned room. He luxuriated in the unaccustomed privacy. Over and over he thanked God for the sudden good fortune until he thought God might get tired of hearing his expressions of gratefulness.

The work was exhilarating. Hard work had never bothered Anis, and he didn't mind feeling important. This was a real job, a good job, a job with a future. He was *somebody*, not just a name on a ration card.

In the evenings he would retire to his room to study his Bible. All his life he had been exposed to the stories and teachings of Scripture. Now the Bible seemed a whole new Book. He was utterly fascinated and set about memorizing long passages just for the pure joy of reciting the sacred words over and over.

He also worked on his English, pronouncing each word precisely, bearing down on every syllable. He knew that speaking well would be essential to advancement in the international firm.

The entries in his diary reveal his change in life and attitude:

> *Tuesday:* I awoke praising the Lord. I praise Him forever because of His great mercy toward me. I believe I am learning my job well. Assad says I am doing even better than he expected.

The oil money had made a prosperous place of the little community that sprang up around H-4. Wealthy customers invited Anis to their homes for parties. There was drinking and dancing, and attractive, friendly girls. Anis declined most invitations, for he feared being drawn into temptations.

He did take advantage of the opportunity to learn to play tennis and developed a real love for the game. After he sat around in the store all day, a strenuous match would leave him feeling exhilarated. It was as much fun as impressing everyone with his prowess at table tennis. But still he felt something was lacking.

"I miss the fellowship with other believers that I had in the Howells' home," he told his diary. "If only there were a church here . . . "

The longing for Christian fellowship persisted along with a yearning to make his life count for God. At H-4 he had everything he had thought he wanted, but something was still lacking. A new dimension had entered his life and sending a good paycheck home each month did not fulfill it.

On days off he went back to Irbid, where he was treated with great respect. He could sense that Samuel looked up to him, and that his uncles were proud of his new status. He enjoyed the prestige, yet the restlessness persisted. There must be something more to accomplish.

He confided in Douglas Howell, "I don't want to seem ungrateful. I really appreciate this job the Lord provided. I have worked there only six months. But I would be happier just serving Him whether I was paid or not."

The Englishman smiled understandingly. "I know how you feel. Perhaps God has something else, something better. I heard the other day that the Gilead Mission hospital in Ajlun has been sold to the Southern Baptists from America, and that the new missionaries are looking for a lab technician. Would you be interested?"

"Working for the missionaries? I certainly would, but what is a lab technician? I know nothing about hospitals."

"They said, 'No experience necessary'; they would train someone. Would you like me to drive you to the hospital? You could find out about it."

"Yes, would you? I would very much appreciate it."

Anis went home and wrote in his diary. "Lord, You are my Refuge. Tomorrow I go to Ajlun and make application there.

Please give me success in my purpose. Be tender toward me . . ."

The next day as they bounced along the rutted, narrow road that snaked through the dry Gilead Mountains, Anis felt extraordinarily happy. Despite the thick dust that billowed around, he sang at the top of his lungs.

After nearly four hours of traveling south on awful mountainous roads, they began climbing the steep hill on which the hospital was built. The road was so dusty they could hardly see the two-story green building until they drove through the front gate of the walled compound. When they stopped, Anis stepped out of the car, brushed the dirt off, and looked around. It was a beautiful location. From this elevation he could see miles into the surrounding valleys, and across to a high peak on which rested the ruins of a 12th-century Crusader castle.

As they entered the hospital building, Anis took a deep breath and breathed a little prayer. Dr. Loren Brown, a tall American with a soft drawl, soon put him at ease with a warm handshake and a friendly smile. After exchanging a few pleasantries, the doctor handed Anis a large medical textbook and said, "Read this page."

Anis read, pronouncing the words phonetically, but not understanding a thing. The vocabulary was entirely new to him, but he continued reading until Dr. Brown interrupted.

"That's fine, Anis. I think you will do. If you want the job I'll train you to do some basic blood work for me. However there are a couple of drawbacks; we can only pay $9 a month, and we are overcrowded in the dorms right now, so for the time being you would have to sleep in a tent. Are you still interested?"

Anis hesitated. He was making $60 a month. This would mean a drastic cut in pay, but he would be working in a hospital, helping heal the sick in the name of Jesus. Then too, he would be with Christians and he truly desired the fellowship of other believers. But could he do it? He hadn't even gone to high school let alone had technical training. But if the doctor was willing, he certainly would try.

"Yes," he answered. "If you will train me, I will work very hard."

"When could you start?"

"I would need about a month, so they could find a replacement for me at Spinney's."

"That will be fine. We'll see you the first of next month."

Anis was thrilled beyond words. This seemed to him such an exciting prospect, but there were many others who thought he had lost his mind. Particularly his friends at H-4. But he went singing along through the next month feeling a peace and contentment in the decision that he didn't quite understand. Was this what it was like to be in the Lord's will? If so, this was the way he wanted to spend the rest of his life. He was so gloriously happy he would fall asleep smiling and wake the same way.

With visions of himself decked out in a white medical coat, walking the halls of the hospital, Anis boarded the crowded, battered old bus that lumbered along the trail that was the main highway to Ajlun. Dr. Brown, who already seemed like a friend, met him and introduced him to the rest of the staff. He was very pleased to be a part of this impressive group.

"Well, Anis," Dr. Brown announced, "I'll show you your first task, so you can get busy bright and early in the morning." He led the new recruit down the dingy steps that led to the dark recesses of the basement. They passed through the huge laundry room where village women on short-legged stools sat bending over the wide-mouthed vats used for cleaning linen in the hospital. Anis stopped long enough to give them all a big smile and to wish them a happy afternoon. Then he followed Dr. Brown into a storage room.

"This will be your lab," the doctor explained a little apologetically. "I'm afraid your first task will be to clean it up so it will be usable."

Open-mouthed, Anis inspected the interior of the long narrow room. It was stacked with charcoal stored in burlap bags that did little to keep the dust from leaking through coarse pores. It looked like a coal pit. *I'm supposed to clean this?* Anis thought, his lip curling disdainfully. *Why, this is a job for a common laborer, not a laboratory technician.*

"Sorry we couldn't have had it all fixed up. The hospital didn't have a lab when we bought it, and this is the only space available. I'm sure you'll have it looking fine in no time."

Anis wasn't quite so confident. His delusions of grandeur quickly melted as he faced the task before him. "Very well," he replied unhappily, "I'll begin first thing in the morning."

That night as he lay on his narrow cot in a little pup tent

he shared with two others, Anis thought of his beautiful air-conditioned room back at H-4. This was quite a come-down. "My son, I've brought you here to learn many things," a Voice said to his conscience.

"Yes, and I came to learn," he grumbled back. "To learn about chemistry, pathology, and blood cells, not how to become a lackey." His dark thoughts continued a few minutes and then he realized, "But I came here to serve You, didn't I, Lord? So if You want me to serve You by cleaning out coal pits, or by digging ditches if necessary, then I will do it. And I will do it happily and with a smile."

Whit this conflict resolved, he rolled over, took a deep breath of the clean mountain air and fell into a sound sleep, unaware that he had already learned a major spiritual lesson.

He awoke to the sound of birds singing merrily around him: they seemed to set the pace for the day. There was time to read his Bible with his tentmates before breakfast, and then chapel services at 7:30. It seemed good to be surrounded by Christians. He felt so happy, he was sure he would burst if he didn't sing. So singing and smiling he set about his task.

He hurried down the stairs into the basement, stopping only to bid good morning to the women already perspiring from the heat of the steam and the energy involved in their endless task. Each beamed a big smile as they returned his cheery greeting. Then he entered the storage room and shouldered the first of the heavy bags of charcoal.

The bags got heavier and heavier as the morning wore on, but Anis continued singing as he worked, spreading sunshine on everyone he met. As the stockroom emptied, the new "lab technician" got dirtier and dirtier. The charcoal dust worked itself through his clothes, until the usually meticulous young man looked like a Welsh collier. But the darker his face, the whiter his smile seemed in comparison.

When Dr. Brown came to inspect progress, he was surprised at the number of bags that had been moved, but even more impressed with the black-faced youth who stood before him. "Anis," he exclaimed, "even your hair looks blacker!"

It took days to clear the room, and then came the scrubbing. He scoured every inch of the room—walls, floor, window ledges, and the high inset windows that were up at ground level. When he finally finished, he felt a real sense of accomplishment. *Now, he thought, this will really be my laboratory, from the ground up.*

Then he and Dr. Brown set to work to make the room look like a laboratory. Surrounded by beakers, glasses, and tubes, Anis felt like a professional. A microscope and an autoclave sterilizer, which Dr. Brown taught him to operate, made his day.

He enjoyed learning from Dr. Brown and even doing research in thick medical books at night. He received satisfaction from doing the most routine tasks. But most of all he enjoyed the Christian atmosphere. Working with Dr. Brown and the other missionaries was for him an honor.

And he learned a lesson that to him was absolutely amazing: money really wasn't all that important. He had thought he was making a great sacrifice in giving up such a good paying job with Spinney's, but had discovered that the Lord doesn't always pay in monetary returns. He now felt joy and peace and fulfillment that could never be attained with mere money.

THE MATURING
OF A MAN

The vengeful Arab—before conversion (early 1951).

The student at Clarke Memorial Junior College (late 1953).

The international evangelist (1975).

The pastor in Jerusalem (1964).

Anis at Ajlun Baptist Hospital, Jordan (1952), using daylight for microscope work (no lights in the lab).

Anis at the Jerusalem airport on his way to America in 1953.

7
THE OPPORTUNITY

The days turned into weeks and a routine was soon established in Anis' life. He would wake early to run with his new friend Suliman Summour in the cool of early morning. They would run through the heavy dew to the privacy of "their" tree on a ridge about a mile from the hospital. There they would read an Arabic translation of B. B. Warfield's *The Lord of Glory*, a study of the life of Christ, and pray.

Then they would race back to the hospital, singing as they ran. Still exhilarated by the run, Anis would meet with Dr. Brown at 6:30 to study. Then to breakfast and chapel. After this Anis would work on the projects Dr. Brown had assigned for the day. In the evenings he worked on his English, which he was determined to perfect.

After a couple of months at the hospital and being around so many Americans all the time, Anis determined to use English whenever possible. "Please speak to me in English," he would say to anyone who could understand. "I want to speak it very well. Please correct me if I make a mistake."

Unable to afford a dictionary, he bought a thick spiral notebook and began making his own list of corresponding Arabic and English words. He also noted the meaning of American idioms which could not be translated literally, such as, "I'm beat" and "Throw in the towel."

All the missionaries were impressed by his self-discipline in study habits and life-style. "I picked a winner, didn't I?" Dr.

Brown declared immodestly to his colleagues, Doctors McRay and Lovegren. They happily agreed.

Dr. Brown was especially pleased with his protégé when he came into the lab and discovered him taking a test. "Where'd you get that, Anis?" he asked.

"Oh, I made myself a quiz to make sure I really understand everything we've covered so far," Anis explained.

"Oh, you did, huh?" Dr. Brown replied. He smiled. "Well, why don't you turn it in to me and I'll grade it for you."

Another day Dr. Brown came upon Anis peering through the microscope so intently that Anis was a little startled when he noticed his mentor looking over his shoulder.

"What're you up to now, Anis?" he asked.

"I'm trying to find this blood type; I think it is B positive."

"Where did you get the specimen?"

Anis grinned and held up a finger.

"Well, let's just see if you're right."

The physician bent over and looked through the microscope. He was pleased to see Anis had correctly identified the specimen.

"Well, Anis, I think you are ready to do blood work."

From then on Anis did all the routine blood typing and as he learned other techniques he took on more and more responsibilities.

Meanwhile, Anis and his friend Suliman were going to nearby communities to share their faith. First they would talk to men on the street, fishing for an invitation to preach in a home. Once this was secured, they would canvass the neighborhood asking people to come.

One evening as they were walking back to the hospital Suliman commented thoughtfully, "People really like to listen to you, Anis. Tonight they were so quiet and attentive as you spoke. Did you ever think God might call you to preach?"

"Me?" Anis asked incredulously. "I just tell stories. I don't really preach. All I do is tell what God has done for me. I don't think I could ever be a preacher."

And yet Anis found it quite natural to witness to others. He would stop and talk to the washerwomen at the tubs, to the laborers out under the trees in the compound, and he always found time to speak to the patients in the wards. He would come to a doorway with his Bible in hand, "Happy afternoon, everyone," he would tell them in Arabic. "I hope you are all feeling better today. May I tell you about Jesus, the great Physician?

"Have you ever thought that perhaps God allowed you to be sick for a short time so you might come here and feel the compassion of these missionaries? They could make much more money in their own country, but they came here to serve so that you might know God loves you.

"The message they bring is that you can be healed in spirit as well as in body. If you find healing for just your body, you will still be sick spiritually and some day you will die. But if you trust Jesus, He will heal your sin sickness."

Everything seemed to be going so well, and then came the scandal that rocked the compound. Anis and a couple of the male nurses were seen playing volleyball with the girls! "They must be communists," the local people decided. "Who else would do such a thing."

To Anis it had seemed such an innocent breach of Eastern culture. The game the nursing students were playing had looked like fun, and before they knew it they were playing too. The female student nurses no longer wore the veil, but were totally separated from the males. At mealtime they went through the same line in the cafeteria, but the men would sit on one side and the women on the other just as they did in church.

The American missionaries weren't too upset at this faux pas, but Dr. Brown counseled Anis to walk more circumspectly in the future. Anis tried to adhere to this admonition scrupulously, but one day a summons came during the middle of the workday.

"The missionaries are having a meeting," an ambulance driver informed him. "They want you there immediately."

What have I done? Anis wondered. *It must be very serious to call me into a staff meeting.* With shaking knees and sweaty palms Anis hurried to the staff room.

Dr. Brown took one look at him and realized how upset he was. "Sit down and relax, Anis; we just wanted to talk to you a minute." Anis sat down, but did not relax.

"We just want to know if you would be interested in going to college?" Dr. Brown continued. Anis blinked in astonishment, not quite understanding what he had heard. "We have received word from Clarke Memorial Junior College in Mississippi that a work scholarship is available for a worthy candidate."

"Missa, Missippi?" Anis tried to repeat.

"Yes, Clarke College in Newton, Mississippi. That's in America, Anis. It's one of our Baptist schools."

"America? You want to know if I'd like to go to America?" he asked loudly, the excitement building up as he realized what they were talking about. "But how could I go to college when I have only finished the seventh grade?"

The missionaries looked at one another blankly. They hadn't realized his lack of formal education, for he had no problem learning the technical aspects of his job. Anis sat on the edge of his chair as the missionaries put their heads together and whispered about the implications of this new information.

Finally Dr. Brown said, "A representative of the college, a minister named Dr. Eugene Keebler, is in Jerusalem now. I think you and I should go and talk to him tomorrow and see if he has any suggestions."

Anis spent a sleepless night. The idea of going to America had never entered his wildest imagination. The thought seemed akin to being translated bodily into heaven. But with no high school diploma, how could he hope to gain a college scholarship?

The following morning, Anis and Dr. Brown climbed into the red hospital jeep behind the driver. Being overtired, and having an empty stomach combined with the swaying of the jeep over and around the steep curves on the trip south, made Anis very sick to his stomach. He no longer worried about meeting the American or the scholarship; now he just prayed fervently, "Lord, please help. Please, Lord. I don't want to disgrace myself in front of my friends."

They started the descent into the Jordan River valley. When Jericho finally came into view, the oasis looked as good to Anis as it had to the 12 spies centuries before. This trip across the Jordan was much less traumatic than the frightening experience five years before when the Shorroshes were running in fear for their lives.

By the time they were nearing Jerusalem Anis was feeling his usual spirited self. His excitement rose as they climbed the steep hill to the city considered holy by multitudes of the earth's inhabitants. The very name Jerusalem means city of peace, but as they entered the city he was disturbed to find many symbols that were the antithesis of the name. It was a sad sight.

They drove by the Mandelbaum Gate, and Anis wanted to stop for a moment and look about. He was surprised to find not a gate at all, but merely a checkpoint for people who wished to "cross over" from one sector of the divided city to the other. Through the barbed wire that formed the wall he could see Israeli soldiers with machine guns, tanks with the fearful Star of David, reminiscent of the loathsome machines that had shattered the peace of Nazareth.

These were the people he had once vowed to kill for taking his home, killing his father, cousins, and other relatives, and for denying his family the right to return to Nazareth and live in peace. God's love had cooled his anger, but he knew there remained thousands of Palestinians, robbed of their homeland, who lived only to exact revenge. The no-man's-land between the two walls of barbed wire reminded him of the gulf that separated his people from the Jews. Could anything or anyone ever bridge that separation? The coexistence that prevailed in 1953 between the two Semitic peoples could hardly be considered a real and lasting peace.

But they had come to Jerusalem for a happier purpose than looking at armaments, so they were off for the American Colony Hotel. The driver pulled into the semi-circular driveway and let Anis and Dr. Brown out under the cupola. Beautiful gardens and flowers surrounded the hotel which had once been a private home. They entered the small lobby and the most beautiful woman Anis had ever seen came toward them. Dr. Brown gave her a warm greeting, then said, "Anis, this is Mrs. Keebler."

"I'm happy to meet you, Anis. Dr. Keebler is waiting for you up in our room," Dorcas Keebler replied in a low, melodious voice.

Anis was so entranced by the sound, he didn't catch the words. He was absolutely awe-struck. This woman was so fantastically ravishing. Her creamy complexion looked as soft and smooth as a flower petal; her huge blue eyes were wide-spaced and sparkling. Her naturally curly blonde hair bounced loosely as she turned toward the doorway expecting the breathless Anis to follow.

He watched, intrigued by the myriad of tiny pleats in her skirt that swayed around her slim body as she walked across the room. *She is more beautiful than any movie star,* Anis thought.

*What a country America must be if even a preacher can afford
to have such a wife!*

It wasn't until they were up in the hotel room and Anis was
introduced to the tall, distinguished-looking Dr. Keebler that he
remembered why he was there.

"You must understand, Anis," Dr. Keebler was saying, "that
you'd have to promise to come back and work in the Middle East."

Anis nodded. He was willing to agree to anything, just for
the privilege of studying in America.

"There's just one little difficulty, Gene," Dr. Brown interrupted.
"Anis has not had the opportunity to complete high school."

The American educator pursed his lips, raised his eyeglasses,
and tugged at the bridge of his nose. He appeared to be studying
the problem while Anis waited impatiently.

"Well," he said at last, "we hadn't anticipated this. But I
suppose we could arrange a high school equivalency course for
him, if he is really God's choice for this scholarship. Let's pray
about it."

As the three Americans knelt to pray, Dr. Keebler nodded
toward Anis to begin the prayer. Anis hesitated for a moment,
because he had never prayed aloud in English before. Falteringly
he began,

"Most loving heavenly Father, I thank You for the miracles
You have done in my life. The greatest miracle of all was that
You loved me enough to die for me. I thank you for revealing
this love to me and for changing my life and giving me purpose.
I thank You so much for these missionaries who have taken an
interest in me and given me a job at the hospital where I can
serve You and my fellowman at the same time.

"Father, if it is Your will for me to go to America, to learn to be
a better lab technician, then I know You will reveal this to us.
But wherever You lead and whatever You want me to do, I
will follow You."

After they had all prayed, they rose from their knees. Anis
was impressed to see Dr. Keebler remove his glasses and wipe
tears from his eyes. The reserved stranger who appeared so imposing at first, now seemed more friendly.

"Well, Anis," Dr. Keebler said, "I guess we'll be seeing you
in the States this fall."

After saying their good-byes Dr. Brown and Anis left. The

anxious youth grasped the physician's arm and asked intently, "What did he say? I don't understand what *fell?*"

"Fell?" Oh, fall. Fall means autumn. He said he expects to see you in the States, in America, in the fall."

"Me?" Anis rolled his eyes and shook his head in disbelief. "He really thinks I will be in America in autumn? Why that's just two months. I am really going? I am?"

Dr. Brown had to assure the overwhelmed young man that he really was going. "It might be better for now if we don't tell anyone until we get all the paper work and red tape cleared up. But we'll start on it right away."

In the days that followed Anis discovered that it was harder to get to America than to get to heaven. He had to have a physical, X rays, passport, visa, certificates of good character, proof of his scholarship, and pass English exams.

Alta Lee Lovegren gave him English lessons each day. She taught him some slang and American colloquialisms she thought he might need in Mississippi.

As the time for departure drew nearer, Anis felt as if he were living in a dream. He confided to his mother and all his family the good tidings. The reaction couldn't have been any greater if he had announced he won a million dollars. Cousins and friends hovered around, patting him on the back and congratulating him. He grinned until his cheeks hurt.

Assad came bringing a couple of suits, a pair of new shoes, and a cardboard suitcase.

Anis went to the American consulate in Amman for his English exams. He did so well that the woman who graded the tests couldn't believe he hadn't finished high school.

Then came the devastating news: The consulate refused to grant a visa for a work scholarship.

"But why?" Anis groaned. "Churches in Mississippi have even donated the funds for my plane ticket."

"I'm sorry," the young diplomatic officer commiserated. "Washington has instructed us that no more visas are to be granted for Jordanians with a work scholarship. Evidently too many are going to the States, getting good jobs, leaving college, and not returning home."

Anis felt totally destroyed. Fortunately the Lovegrens had come into Amman with him. With a hangdog look on his face, Anis meandered back to the hotel where they were staying.

Alta Lee Lovegren took one look at his face and asked, "What happened?"

He explained the catastrophe.

"Let's pray about it, Anis," she suggested. "Maybe something can still be done."

The next three days were pure torture for Anis. Not knowing what would happen and fearing his dream had vanished was the worst mental anguish he had ever known. He couldn't concentrate on his work, on anything; all he could do was pray over and over: "Lord, work a miracle. I believe You want me to go, but You must work a miracle for it to come to pass."

While Anis prayed, the Lovegrens telegraphed Clarke College explaining why his visa had been denied. School officials met, reached a decision, and telegraphed the American consulate in Amman: "FULL SCHOLARSHIP HAS BEEN AWARDED TO MR. ANIS SHORROSH." The consulate notified Anis immediately to come and pick up his visa.

Anis was so overjoyed that he asked two Arab Christian friends, Edward and Khaleel, to join him in prayer and thanksgiving at the mountainside home of a friend who was away on vacation.

While they were praying that night, the room suddenly became bright. They looked up to see a white-clad Man standing in their midst.

Edward crawled into a corner, terrified, and hid his face. Khaleel slid under the bed, shaking convulsively. Anis stayed on his knees overcome by the awesome Presence. He wanted to look at their Visitor, but He was so bright that it was impossible. He closed his eyes in prayer then opened them again. The Visitor was still there, smiling.

Joy flooded Anis' heart. All fear was gone and now he felt elation. It was as though he had been translated into a third heaven by the dazzling Figure he felt assured was Jesus Christ Himself. It seemed a reenactment of the Transfiguration experience witnessed by Peter, James, and John.

All three young men lost track of time, but the Visitor remained. Then finally, sometime after 2 A.M., He began walking past Anis toward the window. As Anis watched in awe, He walked through the iron grillwork behind the window and out into space over the city of Amman. Anis sensed that he was to follow, and in rapt obedience began walking after Him while still on his knees. He had reached the window and was about to climb out when his friends restrained him.

The three were totally overwhelmed by the experience. "What does it mean?" Khaleel asked Anis in reverential wonder.

"He wants me to follow Him," Anis replied confidently.

"Out the window?"

"No," Anis smiled. "He has something for me to do with my life. I don't know what. But I must follow Him, and it will be revealed to me."

8
THE CALLING

September 1953 finally arrived, and it was time for Anis to begin his great adventure. It was hard to say good-bye to all his friends and relatives, especially his brothers, sister, and mother. Em Assad cried and hugged him to her. "I hope I live long enough to see you again," she sobbed as she bade farewell to her son.

Then off to Jerusalem where the magic carpet of Air Jordan was to transport him to a new life. When the twin engines of the DC-3 roared to life, he felt translated to a world of fantasy. He had found a seat next to a window. A lovely young stewardess in a light green uniform with a gossamer veil hanging from her cap, framing her face, came and asked if his belt was fastened. Embarrassed, he clutched his waist, relieved to find it was secure. She laughingly pointed to his seat belt, and showed him how to adjust it.

As the plane started taxiing down the runway Anis' heart began pounding furiously; then, as they left the ground to soar over ancient Jerusalem like a powerful bird, he felt for the first time the exhilaration of flight. Heading north along the Jordan River valley, they soon were flying near the green hills of Galilee. A lump grew in Anis' throat as he strained to see the beautiful land he left five years before.

He thought of Nazareth, just a short distance to the west. So near, yet so very far away. He thought of his grandmother who was now a widow. Would he ever see her again?

He closed his eyes and imagined himself once more in her

big *kharoub* tree. Memory brought back the scent of her aromatic *tabun* bread baking in her outdoor oven. "Come eat, Anis, while the *tabun* bread is still hot," he heard her say.

"Sir, would you have a soft drink?"

He blinked his eyes and nodded. By the time he had finished the Pepsi-cola, they were circling over the blue Mediterranean and preparing to land in Beirut, Lebanon. The first leg of his long journey was over. The next flight would take him to Athens, Greece. Then on to Rome, Copenhagen, London, Glasgow, Iceland, and finally three days later the "milk route" would get him to New York City.

By the time he landed in America Anis had lost track of time on the dizzying flight, but he felt very much the world traveler. Yet even after seeing so many of the great cities of the world, he was awe-struck by the magnitude of New York and the size of the buildings in Manhattan. He spent a night at the YMCA and then decided to play tourist a little while before taking the bus to Mississippi.

What he wanted to see first was the Empire State Building—then the tallest building in the world. He stopped and asked a policeman for directions. "Four blocks to your right," he was instructed. Now he had seen blocks before, they were rectangular cement objects used to make buildings, but he had never thought of them as measuring distance. He looked all around, but couldn't see any—only manhole covers, so he started walking down the street.

He liked New York, he decided. The unbelievably tall buildings that stood like mighty sentinels, the rushing throngs of people scurrying by, the rumble and roar of the traffic, and most of all a feeling of excitement that seemed to ooze from the concrete. And then he looked up and recognized the very building he had been seeking.

He found an elevator and went zooming to the top. From the lofty heights he could see all of the city laid out like a picture postcard. He really was in America, he kept reassuring himself. He spent nearly an hour taking it all in before realizing he was hungry.

Back down on the street he found a cafeteria and went in to get breakfast. He sat down at a table and waited to be served. And waited and waited and waited. He finally decided they had very poor service in America and was about to walk out when he noticed a friendly looking woman and explained his predicament.

"I have just arrived from a very long trip all the way from Jerusalem, and I am very hungry. What must I do to get someone to bring me some food?"

"You just help yourself," the woman smiled. She showed him where to go and indicated the food spread out on the long counter.

"Lady, there is no way in the world I can eat all this," Anis told her, astonished at the quantities available.

"Oh, no," she laughed, "you don't have to eat everything. Or even some of everything. Just pick up what you want and then pay for it at the end of the line."

After putting away a substantial breakfast, Anis went to the bus station to find out when the bus would be leaving for Meridian, Mississippi. "One way or round trip?" the gray-haired man behind the counter asked without looking up. Anis thought it would be nice to go "round" the United States on the way, but didn't feel he had that much time.

"I want a straight ticket," he told the clerk.

"A what?" came the astonished reply and this time the gray eyes of the ticket agent met Anis'. "You want what kind of ticket?"

"I am going to college in Mississippi, so I will need a ticket that will take me straight there," Anis explained.

The man grinned, nodded, and stamped some green pieces of pasteboard. "Here you go, Son. One straight ticket to Meridian, Mississippi."

Though the bus was much slower than flying, Anis figured there were a couple of advantages. The cost was so much less, and it gave him an opportunity to see some of the United States. The only problem he encountered on the three-day trip was the undecipherable menus that were handed him at the quickie food counters along the way. He quickly solved that problem by asking a waitress, "What would you eat at this time of day?" And whatever she brought, he would eat.

When they finally reached Mississippi, Anis was astounded by the fields of white flowers. Acres and acres of white flowers. There were so many he finally spoke to his seatmate about it. "I think all the white flowers are very nice," he ventured, "but why do they grow so many?"

The elderly woman smiled and explained that "those are fields of cotton."

During those first days in the States, Anis came to the conclusion that all Americans must be very friendly. They were always smiling at him.

The people at Clarke College were equally friendly. Anis found the small campus with its towering trees a quiet, placid place. With an enrollment of only 400, he found it easy to make friends among both students and faculty. Especially the Keeblers. Dorcas Keebler was the first to feed him a home-cooked American meal, and he was delighted to find he liked everything.

He was fascinated by all the appliances she used in cooking the meal; he had never seen such a kitchen. Turn a button and instant heat, open a door and instant cold, even an automatic washing machine. He also marveled at other household gadgets that Americans take for granted—blenders, toasters, vacuum cleaners, and electric razors.

But what amazed him the most was the dog in their house.

"Don't you have dogs in your country?" Dorcas asked, amused at his surprise.

"Yes, of course. But only for work," Anis answered. "They keep the sheep and guard the farms, but never would we like one in our house. Don't they . . . well . . . are they clean?"

"Oh, she's housebroken all right," Dorcas laughed. "Not only that, but she thinks she's part of the family. Jezebel," she called. "Jezebel, come here!" The big half-breed, houndy looking boxer got up and ambled to her.

Anis watched as Dorcas put the dog through all its tricks, but the thing that was the most amazing to the new student was the way she talked to the animal and how it understood.

He found having dogs for pets almost as intriguing as another amazing American phenomenon—girls! Girls in the classroom. Girls in the cafeteria. Girls everywhere he looked. All smiling and friendly. How could he ever learn to concentrate with so many girls around?

Anis' course of study included mathematics, science, and a special course called "high school studies." He found it very hard to keep up with the lectures in English, and at first had to look up many of the words the professors used. His vocabulary grew rapidly, however, since he worked on it diligently.

When someone jokingly mentioned that "nice" was the only adjective he knew, he determinedly made a trip to the library to look up some new adjectives in the huge *Oxford Dictionary*. For days after that everything he saw was abundant, adorable, affectionate, agreeable, or amiable. Then they were baffling, beautiful, becoming, or brilliant. Next, colossal, comely, cuddly, or cute as he worked his way through the alphabet.

Anis was "delighted" the first time he was invited to accompany some of his new friends to the local snack shop, the Rainbow Cafe. He put a nickel in the juke box and watched the marvelous machinery that brought forth music. Then he sat on one of the stools at the soda fountain bar and whirled around as he had seen young people do in movies. "This is really living," he proclaimed with a look of total satisfaction on his face.

"What would you like to drink?" he was asked by the freckle-faced young waitress with a perky white cap atop her blond head.

"Coke," he replied, pleased that he had learned the shortened version of the world famous name.

"And what to eat?"

"What do you have?"

"Hamburgers and hot dogs."

"Hot dogs?" he repeated, not believing he had heard correctly.

"Sure hot dogs," one of his chums laughed. "Haven't you ever had one?"

"Well, I want you to know," he explained to his friends indignantly, "that my country is very poor, but never would we eat dogs, hot or cold!" He couldn't help but think of the Keebler's Jezebel, who had become his friend. How could anyone be so cruel as to eat such a trusting animal?

His friends exploded in laughter. They called to the other students in the shop and laughingly explained what Anis had said. He remained adamant in his defense of canines, until someone finally explained to him that hot dogs were not made of dog meat. After they convinced him of this, despite the name, he agreed to try one. All eyes were on him as he took his first cautious bite.

"Hmmmmmm," he proclaimed, raising his eyebrows and giving an approving grin. "That's delicious, delectable, and delightful." He enjoyed the snack so much that he agreed to try another one with chili sauce, and a third. And a fourth. Naturally this got a lot of attention and good-natured kidding, but he enjoyed being the center of attraction. That is, he enjoyed it until he awoke the next morning with an acute stomachache. It got so bad that he was taken to the hospital. At first the doctor thought he had appendicitis, but after running some tests he came back and asked, "Have you eaten anything exotic or unusual recently?"

"Well, I did eat four dogs last night," he replied sheepishly.

"Well, I think you are suffering from acute hot dogitis, but you will recover spontaneously."

News got around in the small town of Newton that there was a Palestinian enrolled in the college and soon he was asked to speak at the local service clubs. One evening he found a notice in the newspaper reading: "Anis Shorrosh, a native of Nazareth, will speak to the Rotary club Monday." Proudly he cut the two lines from the paper and placed them in a scrapbook. It was the first time his name had ever appeared in print.

Anis was flattered to find that Americans were as interested in his homeland and its customs as he was in Americanisms. Girls especially were intrigued by the marriage customs in the Middle East. One lovely young strawberry blonde was particularly taken aback when he explained arranged marriages.

"You mean people really marry total strangers?" she asked suspiciously.

"Yes, indeed. Many men do not see their wives till the day they are married."

"Aw, you're pulling my leg," she replied.

"I . . . what?" Anis stammered, flushing in embarrassment. "Oh, no, I'd never. I've never done anything like that in my life. I assure you, I am most respectful."

Not until she saw how seriously he took her statement did she realize the literal implications of what she had said. Then she had a good laugh. And Anis learned another expression.

One of the most rewarding experiences Anis had at this time came through the international team that was formed to hold special services at various churches. During one of these services, Ron Takimori, a Hawaiian friend of Japanese descent, sang "Jesus, My Pilot Be." As the rich, full notes of his tremendous voice rolled out, "Sometimes when my faith would falter," a bald-headed man, halfway back in the auditorium, rose and stalked out. Anis thought this was strange, for Ron had such a beautiful, powerful baritone.

Then Anis rose to speak. He told of the tragedy that had befallen his family, how despondent and despairing he became, but how Jesus had forgiven him his sins, and given him peace and new life. As he always did in speaking, he told the audience how grateful he was for the opportunity of studying in America.

When he was nearly through the man who had so suddenly left reentered the sanctuary and took a seat on the back row. Another student gave a testimony, then the group sang a song, and an invitation was extended. From the back the large bald-headed man came stumbling down the aisle, tears streaming down his face. Dr. O. P. Moore, the faculty advisor for the group, put his arm around the shaking shoulders, and counseled with the man.

On their way back to the college campus Dr. Moore explained the circumstances. "The Japanese killed that man's son during World War II. He said when Takimori got up there and began singing, he just couldn't take it. He was still so filled with hate, but at the end of the services he prayed and asked the Lord's help in forgiving those enemies. It was really hard for him, but he won a great victory."

The students were all touched, but Anis became very quiet. He lay awake in bed a long time that night, thinking. *I've never really forgiven the Jews for killing my father. I'm not filled with hate as I used to be, but I can't say I have forgiven. Yet the Lord has forgiven me so much. I never really killed anyone, but I would have if I'd had the opportunity.*

Only after a long struggle against his baser emotions was he able to reach the point where he could pray truthfully, "Father, forgive them. I forgive them, help me one day to be able to say I love them."

Now, after only two months, Anis sat with 44 other students to take the college entrance exams. It really wasn't expected that he would pass them after such a short time, but this would give him an idea of what they were like and help prepare him for the next time they were given. Only 18 of the 44 taking the test passed it, and when the list was placed on the bulletin board Anis was dumbfounded to see his name on it. It was like Someone tapping him on the shoulder and saying, "I have brought you to this country because I have something for you to do." He had made straight A's.

More and more opportunities opened for Anis to speak, to

Lions, Kiwanis, and Rotary clubs, as well as churches. He also enjoyed the team weekends when the internationals would spend two days giving testimonies and singing for a church. Often they would have "dinner on the ground," which he found meant a picnic, not literally eating on the ground. Sometimes he accompanied one of the professors, particularly Dr. Keebler, when they spoke at various churches.

The team offerings went to Clarke's scholarship fund. What Anis received for solo appearances was his own, part of which he sent to his mother. He wrote regularly whether he had money to send or not. At times he felt acutely homesick for his family and friends on the other side of the world. He prayed for them daily, along with the missionaries at Ajlun, and for peace and justice in the Middle East.

Anis found strenuous exercise would help alleviate his periodic spells of downheartedness. Tennis and table tennis were his favorites and he excelled in both, but he was always open to new experiences and would accept almost any challenge that came his way.

So when a friend suggested that he try a date, he was quite willing. He had always liked dates. But then he found the word "date" meant more than a fruit, and he was quite hesitant about trying out the new definition. That he liked a certain girl helped. A very pretty redhead who was quiet and shy. He had been attracted to her for sometime, but didn't know how to get to know her better.

He couldn't work up enough courage to *ask* her for a date, so he wrote a letter inviting her to attend church with him. He gave the note to a friend to deliver. Then he waited all day Saturday, anxiously expecting a reply. He was keenly disappointed till he learned that she had gone home over the weekend.

After taking her to church the next Sunday, he decided that dates were so much fun, he started asking girls out two at a time. They would attend church, some school activity, or go for a sandwich and Coke, usually dutch treat. It became a common sight to see Anis strolling across the campus with a girl on each arm.

One adorable young Southern belle invited him to spend the weekend at her home. But when they climbed the steps to her front porch they were met by her father. He took one look at

Anis' dark complexion and reached for a shotgun. He pointed it at Anis and snarled, "Get the_____out of here, and don't let me ever catch you so much as talking to my daughter again."

Anis didn't have to be told twice. He returned to the campus feeling sad, for he felt certain his young friend was very embarrassed by the actions of her parent. This was proved later by the way she avoided him from then on.

Something more serious was troubling Anis very deeply. He finally confided his problem to Dr. Keebler as they drove home one evening from a speaking engagement at a nearby church.

"Dr. Keebler, I am concerned that perhaps I won't be able to fulfill my promise."

"What promise is that?" Gene Keebler asked.

"My promise to return to the hospital in Ajlun and work as a lab technician. I think maybe God is calling me to preach, and I don't know what I should do."

The professor pulled the car over to the side of the road and turned off the engine so they could talk and pray. Anis seemed so concerned and worried, but Dr. Keebler wasn't in the least surprised at what he had been told, and in fact rejoiced in Anis' openness to the call.

"It has been bothering me for the past few weeks," Anis continued. "But I can't understand why God would want me to be a preacher. I am so shy with people, and I am not a good speaker. Why would He call anyone like that?"

"Maybe God just wants you to turn your life over to Him. To be willing to follow no matter where He leads. If He wants you in the ministry, I know He will reveal the way to you clearly. Why don't we pray about it?"

After they had prayed together Anis felt confident that the Lord would reveal His will to him clearly. In the meantime he would just continue to devote himself to his studies.

9

THE PROVIDING

The number one scholastic event at Clarke College was the annual speech contest. Anis decided to enter, using the speech he had given to the various service clubs about the Palestinian problem. To his great surprise and delight, he was chosen as one of the finalists to speak before the student body.

The day for the finals arrived, and with it the five local businessmen who were to act as judges. What Anis didn't know was that one of the men was Jewish.

Anis had only been in the States seven months, and still felt insecure with his limited vocabulary, though some said his grammar was better than most Americans'. But he wanted very much to tell his classmates about the plight of his people.

He stood behind the oversized pulpit, and introduced himself and his topic. "I am Anis Shorrosh. I was born and raised in the hometown of Jesus, Nazareth. Today I would like to give you both sides of the problem that has torn apart the little country of Palestine. Then I would ask you to decide for yourselves on which side truth and justice lie."

The Jewish businessman slid down in his seat and chewed on the end of his pencil. He hadn't expected to be presented with such propaganda. He wished he had never agreed to judge the contest.

"The Israelis say that Palestine rightfully belongs to them, because God gave the land to Abraham and his descendants. The Arabs agree to that statement, but point out that they too are the decendants of Abraham and therefore are entitled to remain in the land they have occupied over the centuries.

"The Israelis point out the vast improvements they have made since they took over the land. The Arabs declare that if the United States and the United Nations had poured as much money and know-how into the country years before, they too could have made the same improvements.

"The Israelis maintain that the United Nations gave them the land, and therefore they are the legal possessors. The Arabs ask, 'Who gave Palestine to the United Nations?' If the U.N. wants to give away land, then let them give land they own, or at least land that is not already occupied."

Anis had warmed to his subject. He no longer was concerned about winning a prize, or even impressing his audience. He just felt an overpowering love and concern for his people who he felt had been so unjustly treated. The passion he felt only made his speech more powerful.

"The Palestinians who were dispossessed nearly six years ago are still living in displaced persons camps and existing on handouts of nine cents a day from the U.N. Can you imagine what it is like to be exiled from your home? To mourn for loved ones who were killed for no reason other than that they lived in a land that was coveted by others? Imagine standing in line for hours waiting for your ration card to be punched so you can receive a measure of flour. Living in tents with no work, no possessions, no hope.

"Each year the General Assembly of the United Nations reaffirms a resolution which states that refugees wishing to return to their homes and live in peace should be allowed to do so. And those who do not choose to return are to be compensated for the loss of their properties.

"The U.N. continues to vote for that resolution, but the years drag by and nothing is done. The Palestinians have become pawns in a situation they had no part in creating. The tragedies that befell the Jews during World War II were not perpetrated by the Palestinians. Why then should they be punished?

"I ask you to choose. On which side are truth and justice? Is there any righteousness in one people displacing another just because they have more powerful friends, more weapons, more sympathy, or more money? I challenge you to choose wisely."

Anis returned to his seat on the platform, his own words still ringing in his ears. He heard nothing of what the next speaker said, though he was very aware that his pronunciation was better and his words more eloquent.

When the contest was over the Jewish businessman took a deep breath. He had to be fair. Right was right. In large, neat letters he wrote, "FIRST PLACE: ANIS SHORROSH."

The results of the voting were not to be released till graduation day some weeks in the future, so Anis and the other finalists had to wait for their decision.

As commencement approached Anis was so busy with exams and term papers that he thought little of the contest. When the big day finally arrived, he was standing at the back of the small chapel with many others, since the room was overcrowded. President Green stood up to announce the winner. "Most significant is the fact that the first prize was won by a young man who is not even a native of our country."

Anis was stunned: he knew he was the only contestant who was not an American. Still he could hardly believe his ears when the president said, "Anis Shorrosh, please come forward." His friends pushed him toward the aisle. All the way down he was patted on the back by well-wishers while the crowd gave him a thunderous ovation.

But clearly above the din of the applause he heard a small Voice asking, "What now, Anis?" He had doubted the Lord's wisdom in calling him to preach, for he didn't think he could ever be a public speaker. Now he had been provided with irrefutable evidence to the contrary. While the audience cheered him, Anis humbly submitted his will to God's. "I will do anything you want, Lord," he pledged.

Winning the contest seemed another miraculous example of God's helping him at a time when he needed help. He liked the $50 prize, too. It seemed God had provided for all his needs. Now if He could just help him overcome his homesickness everything would be perfect.

Even this request was partly granted in a way Anis had not anticipated. He was assigned a new roommate. A young man just over from Jordan! He greeted Sameeh Matalka like a long-lost relative. Just to be able to speak Arabic was so good. And now Anis found himself in the unbelievable position of being the one who was in the know. He took Sam all around, showed him the ropes, and helped him learn some of the colloquialisms that Southerners use.

"You must learn to say, 'Hi, y'all,' " he instructed the newcomer. "It takes a bit of practice to say it just the way they do, but it is worth the effort. Everyone seems very pleased when you can say that just right."

Sam appreciated the advice Anis had to offer, but just the same the two often wound up their teaching sessions with a good wrestling match. Sam was much larger than Anis, but lacked the agility and quickness, so in their wrestling Anis was usually victorious. If all else failed Anis could always overcome his new roommate by tickling him. But to remind themselves that the wrestling matches were just in fun they hung a sign on the wall which read, "A soft answer turns away wrath."

After just 14 months at Clarke Junior College, Anis was ready for Mississippi College, the state senior Baptist College in Clinton. Sam transferred to Mississippi College also, so they were able to stick together at the new school.

By this time word had gotten around that Anis was a good speaker and churches were vying for his appearance. The Baptist Women's Missionary Unions were particularly anxious to hear him, since he was considered a product of Baptist missions. Near Christmastime when the WMUs were promoting the annual Lottie Moon Christmas Offering for Foreign Missions, he had far more invitations than he could accept. The churches where he did speak always exceeded their foreign missions goals.

He always welcomed the money received from speaking honorariums and occasional odd jobs. His scholarship covered the basic essentials of room, board, tuition, and books. Besides needing spending money, he continued to feel responsible for sending a few dollars home to his mother at regular intervals.

His roommate, Sam, could not fulfill the longing which Anis felt for his mother. Anis continued writing her long letters and one evening when he was feeling particularly lonely wrote a tender poem:

> My Dear Mother—My love for thee,
> Wherever thou may be,
> Beyond the great mountains
> Or across the murmuring seas.

They tell me, motherly love is the truest love,
And I think they've gotten the right idea.

To me, you are my life, my light, and love.
Remember the one who is away,
Remember him whenever you pray,
Morning, night, or in the noonday.

I shall wait . . . and pray . . . and prepare
Till the day comes, Oh! What a day!
We shall meet,
Maybe not here,
But if so, I am sure up there.

At Mississippi College he continued making good grades, although he nearly drowned himself because his Arab pride would not let him admit he couldn't swim. This was one of the few things he had ever determined to learn and could not.

One of his favorite courses was driver education. He loved the feeling of power that came from controlling the many horse-powered engines. Then too, his practical side realized the value of being able to get where he needed to be without always depending on others to provide transportation or hitchhiking. He decided to demonstrate just how Americanized he had become by buying a car on credit.

His first selection, a vintage Oldsmobile, cost $413. When it fell apart within two weeks, the salesman repented and let him apply his down payment toward a newer car, a shiny black Ford, just two years old. Anis felt like a king driving the '53 auto back to the dorm, and that night wrote in his diary:

Thank you, Lord! It is a thrilling experience to have
a car of my own, but I hope it won't make me have pride.
I am glad, but a little worried because many will think
I am too rich and maybe Dr. Keebler won't like that.
It is coming very handy during this study course, "The
Moslem World," for I have engagements all the time.

Frequently, when he was introduced, people would be shocked to meet an Arab who was a Christian. After getting over their surprise, they would make such comments as, "I thought all Arabs worshiped Mohammed," or, "I didn't know there were Arabs who believed in Jesus." Anis would smile and explain, "Most Arabs are Muslims, or as some say 'Moslems,' but at least 10 million belong to Christian tribes. That doesn't mean they are true believers, but they are at least Christian by tradition. Ten percent of the population of Jordan and Syria is Christian. Egypt is about 17 percent Christian and Lebanon 50 percent. You see, God loves Arabs, too."

At Mississippi College, as at Clarke, fellow students were curious about the Muslim culture which dominated the Middle East. They would say, "Tell us about Mohammedanism," and Anis would point out that "Arabs are insulted if you call them 'Mohammedans.' They insist that they worship God only and that Mohammed was only His prophet. The correct terms are 'Islam' and 'Muslims.' "

Questioning that often began with only one or two students would attract a crowd to Anis' dorm room, or around a table in the dining room. There was nothing Anis liked better than an attentive audience, especially one interested in Arabian culture and religion.

Such informal talks resulted in invitations to speak to sociology and missions classes.

"Anyone desiring to present the Christian faith to Muslims," Anis would advise, "should first know what Muslims believe, not what many Christians think they believe. *Islam* means 'submission,' and Muslims are supposed to be ones who submit to God. Muslims claim no divine or supernatural powers for the prophet Mohammed. They believe that God selected him to teach His message, that he was the last of the prophets, and that he was a model for their conduct.

"Mohammed was born in Mecca in A.D. 570. He was supposed to have communicated with God for the first time in 610. Not many know, however, that just before that time he went to Damascus and was influenced by a group of Docetists. If you remember your church history, you know that the Docetists did not believe in the divinity of Jesus. One of Mohammed's teachings was that Jesus was not divine, but only another great prophet like Moses.

"The Koran is something of a synthesis of parts of the Bible and some of the ideas Mohammed supposedly received by revelation. Mohammed's main emphasis was that there is only one God. Consequently, he persuaded the people of Mecca to destroy all their idols. After the statues and images were cleared out, Mecca became the Islamic center of worship which every devout Muslim tries to visit at least once during his lifetime.

"Mohammed's followers consolidated the Arab tribes and embarked on a holy war against idolaters. Since Mohammed taught that any warrior killed in a holy war would go straight to paradise, Arab soldiers fought fiercely.

"They spread their religion and language across North Africa. They invaded Europe in 711, and on the Rock of Gibraltar Tarik ibn Zaid, the Arab general, delivered a speech to his troops which every Arab must learn: 'The sea is behind you, the enemy before you, you have nothing but faith in Allah and patience in this battle. Therefore attack, and we shall win the victory.'

"They marched across Spain and crossed the Pyrenees into France before Charles Martel finally stopped them at the historic Battle of Tours in 732. For the next 500 years the Islamic Empire was the greatest power in the world. The Arab influence in Spain is still seen in Moorish architecture, music, and culture. The Moors were not forced out of Spain till 1492, a date which is known to you for another great event. Today there are almost half a billion Muslims in the world, around 20 times the number of Baptists. Not all are Arabs, of course.

"Islam is not as foreign to what we believe as you might think. Consider their five pillars: One, witnessing to the oneness of God; two, praying at least five times daily; three, giving alms; four, fasting during the month of Ramadan; and five, Hedj, a holy pilgrimage to Mecca.

"But Muslims do not approve of Christianity because they think we worship three Gods, Father, Son, and Holy Spirit. Five times every day they proclaim, 'There is no God but Allah, and Mohammed is His prophet.' However, they no longer fight holy wars because the day of the great warriors is long past. If my people, the Palestinians, had been soldiers instead of farmers and shepherds, they would never have been driven from their land by the Jews.

"The plight of the Palestinians is now a shame to all the Arab nations. They are mobilizing so they will never suffer such humiliation again. I am very sorry that I cannot prophesy peace for the Middle East. I fear the worst is yet to come."

Most could not understand why Anis was so serious much of the time. "Come on and play basketball," they would say. But if he hadn't finished his assignments for the day he would merely smile thanks and return to his books. The tragedies which had happened to his family and his people had matured him beyond his years. The years he had longed to attend school and couldn't made him appreciate the privilege of an education, which so many of his fellow students took for granted. Most of all, he was pursuing a calling which had been deeply embedded into his soul.

His studiousness allowed him to accomplish an amazing feat. In just 33 months he had completed requirements for both a high school diploma and a college bachelor of arts, majoring in English and sociology.

As graduation day approached in 1956, he reflected on all that he had learned since coming to the United States. It seemed many important parts of his education had come not through classes, but through people and circumstances. There had been times when he had gone hungry, but true to his Arab heritage, he had never told anyone that he was in need. God had always provided.

There had been times when he didn't have money for a haircut, and felt embarrassed to have long hair. Yet each time he had been "short," he had learned to trust God. Now he had scores, even hundreds of friends, and a car of his own. Only one lack marred his happiness on Graduation Day. His beloved mother could not be there to see him receive his college diploma.

He asked someone to take his picture so that he might send it back to Jordan. He swallowed hard and blinked rapidly as he envisioned his mother showing it off to all the relatives. How he missed her, his whole family, and his friends and relatives. But there was no way he could afford a visit, and he felt compelled to continue his education at the New Orleans Baptist Theological Seminary.

If God was calling him to be a preacher, then he must get the best training. He couldn't shake the feeling that he must prepare to meet the destiny the Lord had mapped out for him.

Anis delivering his prize-winning speech at Clarke Memorial Junior College, Newton, Mississippi, May 1954. President William Green of Clarke seated behind him.

Anis with Silvia Goberia (Brazil) and Direk Arayakasol (Thailand), Mississippi College, Clinton, January 1955.

The popular Anis with foreign students Jachin Chin from Hong Kong (left), "Nick" Alexandrenko from Russia, and John Kondo from Japan (standing, right) at New Orleans Baptist Theological Seminary in 1958.

Nell Martz,
student nurse,
1956.

Twins Ann and
Nell Martz.
Which did Anis marry?

Nell at engagement shower with her Jordanian
"wedding present."

Mr. and Mrs. Anis Shorrosh, newlyweds, August 31, 1957.

10
THE ROMANCE

When Anis reached New Orleans in September 1956, he found that the seminary was still in the process of moving across town to a new campus. He had to live in the "old" men's dorm in the Garden District and attend classes on the new Gentilly campus. Since he had a car, he ferried other students back and forth and picked up extra gas money.

In August Egypt had angered the British and French governments by nationalizing the Suez Canal. At the same time Israel and her Arab neighbors were skirmishing along their borders. Anis' fears that his family was in danger increased in early September when Israel made bloody "reprisal" raids into Jordan and Syria. He kept the radio on while driving to and from classes.

One morning in October he was driving to the new campus when a fellow student asked if he would make a stop at Charity Hospital and pick up three nursing students who wanted to visit the seminary.

The three young women climbed into his car just as the latest Middle East news was being flashed. Anis didn't mean to be rude, but he was so absorbed in the report that he didn't even look up when the girls were introduced.

The broadcast ended just as he was pulling up for a red light at the corner of Claiborne and Canal Streets. He flipped off the radio and turned to glance at the new passenger sitting beside him. He almost stopped breathing for a minute as he looked into a pair of the most beautiful blue-green eyes he had ever seen. His lovely, dark-haired companion smiled and said, "Hi," and he thought, *This is the one! This is the girl I want to marry.*

He was brought back to reality by honking horns and a sarcastic call, "Green means go, Anis," from the back seat. He didn't say much the rest of the trip, but tuned in to every delicious word that fell from the well-shaped lips of Nell Martz.

When they reached the campus he asked if she had had breakfast.

"Oh, we've already eaten," she replied sweetly. "But we could have another cup of coffee."

The seven young people went through the cafeteria line together, but Anis managed to slide into a seat next to Nell when they found a table. He never enjoyed a meal more.

"How about attending some classes with me, and I'll show you around the campus during breaks," he suggested. She smiled and shook her head. To his consternation, she already had made plans for the day and wasn't even free to eat lunch with him.

It didn't take much asking around to get the phone number of the Charity Hospital nurses dorm, and that afternoon as Nell entered her room, the phone was ringing. After turning on the charm for a few minutes, Anis asked for a date that evening. She was a little surprised, and very flattered, for she had heard other nursing students talk about the dashing young Arab seminarian, and any number of them would have loved to have such an invitation.

"That sounds like fun," she replied. "Why don't you pick me up about seven?"

"I shall be there early in anticipation of seeing your lovely face again," he replied with his Rudolph Valentino charisma.

After an enjoyable time in the city, Anis suggested that they drive out to the seawall on Lake Pontchartrain and watch the nightly submarine races.

"Submarine races?" Nell asked incredulously.

"Oh, yes," Anis replied, tongue in cheek, "they are all the rage, I understand."

So they drove to the lakeshore and walked out to the cement steps that formed the protective seawall. The moon was nearly full and the reflection on the choppy water made a very romantic setting. There was just enough moonlight to set off the new pale blue skirt and sweater set Nell was wearing.

Anis took her hand and gave her a dazzling smile, "You are the most adorable, bewitching, captivating, delightful girl I have ever met," he proclaimed. He had long since graduated from dictionary study and was now at work mastering a thesaurus. "I want you to tell me all about yourself. Everything that has ever happened to you, so that I might have the enchanting opportunity to hear your musical voice."

Nell smiled impishly. "Well, I'm from a small town in Alabama, Enterprise, where my father is pastor of the Park Avenue Baptist Church. I'm a student at the Baptist School of Nursing in Birmingham and came to Charity Hospital here in New Orleans for three months of special pediatric training. I play the piano, and like swimming and tennis.

"I have an identical twin sister, Ann, who is married to a preacher, Louis Reynolds. And a younger brother, Richard."

"You have an identical twin? How interesting, but then I should have guessed it. When the Lord made you, He must have been so pleased that He decided to make two of you. Is your sister training to be a nurse also?"

"Oh, such flattery," Nell responded and laughed. "No, we started out in Howard College in Alabama together, but I felt the Lord wanted me to be a nurse, so I entered prenursing and she is majoring in education. When I went to nursing school we broke up for the first time. I do miss her.

"My family is really pretty neat. Father has always worked with mission-type churches; in fact he has built four or five churches. My mother had always wanted to go to China as a missionary; they have both been very much interested in missions. So they understand my call to missions."

"Ah, if you want to be a missionary, perhaps you would be interested in learning some Arabic?"

"Oh, yes. I've never even heard Arabic. Do teach me something."

"Very well. *'Anna bahibback.*"

"*'Anna bahibback,*" she repeated haltingly.

"Ahhhhh," Anis sighed. "I like that. Say it again."

"But what does it mean?"

"Oh, never mind. It's something nice. Just say it again. I love to hear you say it," he replied, hesitant to tell her it meant "I love you."

She repeated it a couple more times, then asked to be taught something else.

"Try, *'Ay teni bousa.'*"

She said that a few times, but demanded to know what it meant. He slid over close to her, put his arm around her, and whispered, "It means 'give me a kiss.' " And he kissed her.

"One thing more you must learn," he requested. *"Aiwa*; it means 'yes.' "

"Aiwa, that's easy. How do you say no?"

"Oh, I'll never tell you," Anis laughed. "I want you always to say *aiwa* to me."

"Right now, I must tell you it is time to take me back to the dorm. They are very strict about curfew."

When they pulled up in front of the dorm, a few minutes remained before curfew, so they sat and talked until the last possible moment. When Anis asked to see her again the next night, she replied, *"Aiwa,"* with a big smile.

Anis spent a sleepless night thinking of the captivating Nell. What beauty. And grace. And poise. And her delightful, infectious laugh. And best of all, she was a dedicated Christian who was already planning on serving the Lord on the foreign field. *What better place than Jordan,* he thought. When he returned to Ajlun to work at the hospital as he had promised, wouldn't the missionaries be delighted if he brought along a nurse?

He found it impossible to concentrate that day. The professors were boring. The hours seemed to linger on and on. For some reason he even lost his appetite. He was waiting in the lobby of her dorm early, anxiously eyeing each student who left the elevator. At last the doors opened to reveal his long-awaited date.

"My dear, you look positively ravishing this evening," he greeted her with a big smile. He took her hand and led her out of the dorm and to the car. "I must confess that you have completely bewitched me. You have so dazzled me that I can think of nothing else. I thought tonight would never come."

The time together went all too quickly, and they had to make a mad dash to get her in before curfew. To his great chagrin, Anis had to say that he already had promised to preach for a church in northern Louisiana that weekend and wouldn't be able to see her till Monday.

Saturday and Sunday were an exquisite torture for him. He

missed her so much, yet enjoyed the pain that thinking of her brought. When he got back to New Orleans late Sunday night, he had to call her. "I'm scheduled to speak to the nurses at their chapel services tomorrow night," he told her. "Could we perhaps go someplace afterward?"

They could.

This was Nell's first opportunity to hear Anis speak. She found him forceful, compelling, and thought-provoking. She was proud that he had selected her from all the student nurses to take out.

They walked across the street to a drug store and ordered Cokes. Anis told her about his weekend and how much he had longed to see her. Then he asked how she had spent her time.

"I went to a football game at Tulane University, and then we went to dinner."

"We? Who did you go with?" Anis demanded indignantly.

"Oh, with a young civil engineer I've been dating. We had a very nice time."

"Girl! You are breaking my heart! I thought you were serious, as I am. We're going to get married; you can't date anyone else!"

"Anis, you are crazy," she exclaimed as she laughed. "This is only the third time in your life that you have ever seen me."

"My parents met only once before they were engaged. My brother-in-law saw my sister only one time and he knew she was the one for him. And I know assuredly that you were meant to be mine."

With this pronouncement he pulled his prized possession, his college graduation ring, from his finger and grabbing her hand, tried to push the ring on her finger.

"Anis, no," she protested, pulling her hand free. "We don't know each other well enough. And I don't know if I even want to go steady with anyone right now. I've been hurt before, I don't want to get serious. Can't we just be friends?"

"Friends!" he snorted. "My beloved, you are much more than any friend can ever be. Already you are the very center of my existence. How could I ever contemplate life without you?"

Nell continued her protest, but Anis was just further enticed by the challenge of the pursuit. He proceeded to date her every night. The dash to beat curfew hour became a regular thing as it became harder and harder for them to say goodnight.

During this time Nell saw the serious side of Anis. He confided his worries about the worsening Middle East situation and his apprehensions about the safety of his family. "The *New York Times* says Egypt and Iraq may invade Jordan," he said. "And that Israel is mobilizing its troops!"

The next evening he came dashing into the dorm a few minutes late. "Did you hear the news?" he asked Nell breathlessly. "Israel has invaded the Sinai Peninsula! The raids on Jordan where my family is were just diversionary."

Two nights later: "The British and French have gone into Egypt to regain control of the Suez Canal."

Two days after this: "They say it's all over. Israel has taken the Gaza Strip and the entire Sinai Peninsula. And Israel's ambassador to this country, Abba Eban, said less than a week ago that Israel would start no war."

Nell listened and said nothing all the way to the car. By the time they had driven to the lakeshore, Anis was more relaxed. At least he now seemed less worried about his family.

Concern over Arab-Israeli hostilities did not dim his ardor for Nell. Two weeks from the time they had first met, he very formally and properly asked, "Nell, Sweetheart, will you marry me?"

And she replied sweetly and succintly, "No."

Of course this discouraged him not in the least, and he went home, got a discount catalog, and ordered her a ring by mail. It took another week of persistence to change the "no" to "yes." This was at Thanksgivingtime, and he hoped for a brief engagement with marriage at Christmastime, but Nell wanted to finish her training with her class and would not graduate till the following August.

During the Christmas holidays Anis went home with Nell to Enterprise, Alabama to get to know her parents. When he asked for her hand in marriage, Otto Martz gave a resolute "no." The Martzes were not prejudiced against him because he was a foreigner, but the idea of becoming engaged after such a short time shocked them. After all, Nell's twin had gone steady with Louis for two years, and had been engaged for four years before she married.

The Martzes were impressed with Anis' sincerity and his devotion to Nell during the weekend he spent in their home. Nell's maternal grandmother, Annie Hodges, was also there at that time, and, in accordance with Arab custom, Anis was very gracious to the elderly woman. He held her chair, waited on her, told her complimentary little nothings, and in general, completely charmed her.

Before the two started back to New Orleans Sunday evening, Nell's grandmother took her aside and whispered, "Marry him, Nell. Marry him!"

Despite the lack of parental blessing, Nell accepted the ring, and they considered themselves officially engaged.

Toward the end of December Anis and Nell drove to Nashville, Tennessee for the Southern Baptist Student World Missions Congress. Thousands of students had gathered from all over the country. The huge War Memorial Auditorium was the largest Anis had ever seen. Anis' expenses were paid by the congress because he was to be one of the speakers. The program committee gave him 10 minutes to speak on "America in the Eyes of the World," just before Billy Graham spoke.

When Anis' time to speak came, he was introduced as "A product of Baptist missions who has done us proud. Born in Nazareth, now a Jordanian citizen . . . his native tongue is Arabic, but he will address you in English." The man ran on and on, painting a portrait of an intriguing foreigner. When he finally said, "And now I present to you, Anis Shorrosh," Anis walked behind the big pulpit, shuffled his feet in a modest gesture of nervousness, then flashed a wide smile and said, "Hi, y'all," in his best Southern drawl. It brought the house down. The crowd convulsed in laughter.

"People all over the world are watching America," he began after the audience had settled down. "They are wondering if the Gettysburg Address is a reality, or has it been forgotten." He had practiced and practiced the forceful speech so that he could give it without notes, but when he concluded with a ringing flourish, he was shaken to see people getting to their feet.

Have I offended them? he wondered in dismay. *What could I have said that would make them walk out?* Then he realized no one was leaving; they were standing and clapping. The thunderous applause reverberated across the auditorium and even though Anis had never seen a "standing ovation" before, he realized that he was receiving a vote of approval.

After the first of the year Nell had to return to Birmingham to complete her training and the romance was continued by mail. They did get to see each other occasionally on weekends, and had "dates" by phone at other times.

As they had time to get to know Anis, Nell's parents came to accept him, and by spring they were looking forward to having him as part of their family. Even though Anis could not demonstrate his ability to support their daughter, he knew that the Lord had always supplied his needs, and could see no reason why He would not provide for two. Happily, the Martzes had themselves lived by faith long enough to agree with him.

The wedding was set for August 31, after Nell's graduation from nursing school. Anis arranged for the invitations to be printed in Jerusalem, so they could be done in both English and Arabic. He wanted to send his relatives an invitation even though he knew they could not come to America for the joyous event.

Since Park Avenue Church in Enterprise had no organ, the larger facilities of the First Baptist Church were reserved. Nell's father and Dr. B. R. Justice of First Church, a good friend of Neli and Anis', were asked to officiate.

Anis wished so much his mother could attend, but since that was impossible, he asked a dear friend and benefactor, Mrs. Ollie Richardson, if she would take Em Assad's place.

As the wedding preparations moved ahead, Anis chuckled to friends about the difference in Arabian and American wedding customs. "In my culture the groom does almost everything," he said. "All the bride has to do is show up for the wedding. I sure am getting off easy."

It was hectic for poor Nell who had much more to do than "show up" at the church. Just two nights before the wedding she graduated from her nursing course and also received a $100 scholarship for being the outstanding Christian student nurse of her class. Her B.S. was to be awarded later, since Howard College did not graduate in the summer. That same week she was given a shower that Anis had a hand in planning.

Nell's friends had written to Anis to ask what would be an appropriate gift for a Jordanian country bride. He had replied that "no self-respecting Jordanian country girl would get married without having either a camel or a goat." Since camels were not readily available in Alabama, they borrowed a goat from a neighbor with a dietary problem.

Nell was opening gifts during the shower when the doorbell rang. There stood a pseudo-telegraph messenger and a "telegram" from the "Arabian Government." The "telegram" stated that Nell Martz was to receive a goat for milk and transportation as a wedding gift. Then they led in the bleating animal. As Nell almost collapsed in surprise, a photo bulb flashed. The "joke" along with her picture made the front page of the *Birmingham News*.

The big day, August 31, 1957, dawned bright and beautiful. The chancel was decorated with magnolia leaves and graduating candelabra and baskets of white gladioli and mums. Ann Reynolds, Nell's twin was the matron of honor and wore a beige chiffon dress over taffeta, as did the three bridesmaids. They carried bouquets of yellow roses.

Anis, handsome in his summer tux with white jacket, stood with his groomsmen anxiously awaiting his bride. The other girls were all gorgeous, and of course the matron of honor was a duplicate of his bride, but that day he had eyes only for Nell. At last she entered the sanctuary on the arm of her father. She looked radiant in her lace and tulle white gown with a lace Victorian collar. The bouffant tulle skirt was accented by a lace peplum and her fingertip veil of illusion fell from a Juliet crown of rose-point lace.

Anis could only thank God for such a wife.

Following the ceremony, there was a reception in the church fellowship hall. Then Nell changed to her mauve pink dress for their wedding trip into the mountains. After much hugging and kissing, congratulating, and the throwing of the bridal bouquet, the newlyweds raced to Anis' Ford under a shower of rice.

With his usual penchant for orderliness, Anis had planned their honeymoon to the last detail. They would drive the four or five hours to Atlanta that evening, spend one night there, then go to Gatlinburg, Tennessee in the Smokies the next day. He had prepared a list of activities and sights they should see along the way. And he had even packed a chess set, for he wanted to teach his bride to play.

But. They drove to the first motel. Took several nights to get to Gatlinburg. Never looked at the list. Forgot all about the chess set. And had a glorious honeymoon.

11
THE DISAPPOINTMENT

After their honeymoon Nell and Anis set up housekeeping in a one-room efficiency apartment on the seminary campus. They felt very "married" after making their first trip to the grocery store together. The 54 items came to a total of $14.73. After stacking the foodstuffs in the tiny cubbyhole that served as a kitchen unit, Nell pasted the sales slip in her bride's book.

In adjusting to living together Nell learned that Anis was very sensitive to the least criticism from her. He felt his wife should be his staunchest supporter, and never reveal any of his faults to others. But he wouldn't get angry or shout when displeased; instead he would sit silently and sulk.

One day while Nell was cleaning the kitchenette she told him, "Anis, you have to take out this garbage; it's running over."

"I what?" he asked, incensed that she should give him an order. "You have to take out the garbage," she repeated innocently.

He seethed for a few seconds, the outrage of such a command causing his blood to boil. Then he stalked out the door, slamming it behind him. He marched briskly across the grassy field that separated the apartments from the library.

Still indignant, he walked into the library and found a couple of books on the required reading list of one of his courses. Then he entered the reading room and sat down at a table to study.

He stared blankly at the pages before him. "The nerve, the audacity of that girl. Ordering me around like that. Doesn't she know I would do anything in the world for her if she would just ask me nicely? I am good to her. I try to please her. And now she takes advantage of me by trying to boss me around.

"Well, I'll show her who is head of our family. I will make her beg and apologize and promise never to do it again. But I will remain aloof. I shall not kiss her, or even speak to her for a week. I have to teach her from the very first that I am not a peon to be ordered around. I will be master in my own house."

He continued glowering at the pages of his book as the dark thoughts raced through his mind. He was determined to punish his wife for this insult to his manhood.

After more than an hour had passed he glanced toward the swinging doors that opened to the wide foyer. Through the glass windows he saw Nell peering in. He returned to his book, pretending he had not seen her distraught face. She entered the room and came and stood next to him; still he ignored her. Then she sat down in the chair beside him. He gave her absolutely no recognition.

Blinking back tears, she placed a hand on his arm and whispered in a choked little girl voice, "Honey, aren't you coming home?" He turned and looked at those beautiful pleading eyes, and all the anger in him melted. How could he stay angry at such an adorable creature? They walked back to the apartment arm in arm. Having survived their first "fight," they learned how much fun it was to make up.

Nell used her scholarship money to enroll in some New Testament courses and took organ lessons. She also worked part time at the Baptist hospital in New Orleans.

One day she returned home from work to find Anis slumped down in a chair staring morosely into nothingness. "What's wrong, Honey?" she inquired.

"Oh, nothing. I was just thinking about the chapel address this morning. The speaker was talking about humility. Nell, I have to admit, I am not humble. I would like to be, but I'm just not.

"As a matter of fact," he continued, warming to the subject, "I would like to be the *most* humble man in the whole world."

This reduced Nell to giggles. At first Anis was startled by her reaction, then he realized just what he had said and joined in her laughter. "See," he said, turning up his hands and shrugging, "it's impossible."

"Well, you can't excel in everything, Anis," she consoled him.

"The Lord has given you your personality and you just have to do the most with what you have."

"Yeah, I guess you're right," he agreed and pulled her on his lap for a welcome home kiss.

Anis preached almost every weekend, traveling throughout Louisiana, Mississippi, Alabama, and Georgia, but because of her work Nell couldn't always accompany him. Their second year on campus, 1958-59, she had an even better reason; she was expecting. Anis' joy was boundless.

During that year Dr. Leo Eddleman, the missionary who had meant so much to him during his boyhood days in Nazareth, was elected president of the New Orleans Seminary. It was so good to be reunited with him and his wife, Sarah, after so many years.

Nell continued working till the eighth month of her pregnancy. They needed the money. Only at Clarke Memorial College had Anis received a full scholarship. At Mississippi College and at the seminary he had, except for the help of a few friends, been paying his own way.

Besides preaching, selling reading/writing clipboards to fellow students, and carrying a full course load, Anis held down a job as assistant to Dr. Roy Beaman, the seminary's resident archaeologist. From Dr. Beaman Anis acquired a love for the past in the lands where he had grown up. He wished he had appreciated the antiquities that surrounded him in his youth which he had just taken for granted. Now he looked forward to receiving his Bachelor of Divinity and returning to the Middle East.

Both Nell and Anis had been working to fulfill the requirements of the Southern Baptist Foreign Mission Board for appointment as missionaries. So they eagerly looked forward to a conference with a board representative in the spring of '59 before graduation.

The man asked them to meet him at a Baptist conference on the Mississippi Gulf Coast. Nell was in no condition to make the trip, so Anis went alone. Both expected that the representative would tell them what final preparations they needed to make before appointment.

"I feel a little embarrassed at having to tell you this, Anis," the representative began gently. "I know how much you have done for the Foreign Mission Board through your speaking over the past years. We have had excellent reports on the money you have raised for the Lottie Moon Christmas Offerings, and how you have always promoted the denominational Cooperative Program.

"Now that you are almost through seminary, I realize you will have fulfilled all the academic requirements the Board has for its candidates, but we will not be able to appoint you."

Seeing the surprised look on Anis' face, he hastened on. "The board has a policy not to appoint foreign nationals. I know this policy sounds unfair to you, and I regret you did not know about it earlier. And since Nell is married to you, we won't be able to appoint her either. I'm sorry but this policy is on the books and we must abide by it."

Anis sat quietly, thinking, saying nothing, still stunned. He was soon to receive his second degree from a Baptist institution. He already spoke the language of the people he wished to serve and was completely acculturated in their customs. Surely he would be a good representative for Southern Baptists in Jordan, but if they couldn't send him, he would just depend on the Lord to provide another way.

"What we can do, Anis," the man continued kindly, "is hire you as a native pastor. This way you can work for the missionaries and meet your scholarship agreement. The salary is very low, but it would be something. And if Nell will teach the nurses in Ajlun we could pay her transportation."

It was a disappointing blow, but Anis accepted the situation. He knew that a native Arab pastor was paid only $145 a month, and that it would be difficult for three people to live on that amount. "Thank you," he said. "We will appreciate the Board's help with transportation costs. And don't worry about us. I have lived by faith for a long time now; the Lord will provide," he consoled the distressed-looking man. Then before leaving, Anis signed an agreement to work for the Baptist Mission in Ajlun for at least three years.

"Well, I wanted to be humble," Anis told Nell when he returned home. "This has certainly taken some pride from me. After working so hard these years and making good grades I will go back on the same level as the national pastors with no training."

Nell wasn't particularly distressed with the setback. She was willing to look to the Lord for their needs, but her parents were upset.

"With a baby coming, how will your family exist on such a low salary?" Emma Martz asked. "We've known for years, Nell, that you would be going as a missionary. We just never considered that you wouldn't be appointed by the Board."

"I'm sorry about that," Anis replied, crestfallen.

"Well, it certainly isn't your fault," Otto Martz said in Anis' defense, "but you can understand our concern."

"Yes, but Daddy, we already have some friends who have promised to help us. Don't worry. Everything will work out fine. The Lord will take care of us."

Both Nell and Anis continued to feel peace and confidence as three big events approached. First, Anis was ordained to the ministry on April 22 by the First Baptist Church, New Orleans. Next, Dr. Eddleman presented him with his seminary degree, extending him congratulations in Arabic. And most exciting of all was the birth of their firstborn, who arrived on May 21.

Anis was ecstatic over the safe delivery of his beautiful son, and immediately sent a cable to his mother in Jordan. Since he would be known for the rest of his life as the father of his eldest son, he and Nell prayed and thought long and hard about a name. They finally settled on Salam, which meant "peace." Anis would now be called, Abu Salam, "father of peace." A good name for one whose calling was to proclaim the Good News of the Prince of Peace, he felt. Because Arab custom is also to make the middle name of a baby the father's first name, the child's birth certificate read Salam Anis Shorrosh.

Near the end of June they started on the long awaited trip back to Jordan, ending nearly six years of American study for Anis. They stopped off first in Enterprise to give Nell's parents the opportunity to see their first beautiful, bouncing grandchild. Then they motored to New York to set sail on the S/S *Cleopatra*. The faithful '53 Ford which Anis had bought in Mississippi was put on board with them.

On a Monday evening, July 13, the *Cleopatra*, flying an Egyptian flag, left the docks and sailed past the Statue of Liberty. Anis and Nell stood on deck and watched the Freedom Lady grow smaller and smaller in the fading sunset. Salam was not in the least impressed with the view, and demanded food. Immediately.

The ship sailed smoothly the first couple of days, then on the 16th was buffeted by strong winds and began to rock uncomfortably. Anis was one of several passengers who skipped dinner.

But he soon recovered and by Sunday was able to hold a preaching service on board with Nell playing the piano.

Every evening they moved their watches up 30 minutes as the ship sailed steadily eastward. When they entered the Mediterranean, they noticed that the vessel kept zig-zagging for no apparent reason. After docking at Beirut, they learned why. The Egyptians had seized an Israeli ship and the Israelis were looking for an Egyptian ship to retaliate.

They spent the night in Beirut, then drove south and connected with the famous Damascus Road. They stopped one night en route and finally, hot, tired, and weary, pulled into Irbid.

When Anis stopped the car in front of his mother's home, relatives came upon them from all directions. Em Assad got to her son first. "How I have waited and prayed for this day," she exclaimed as she hugged and kissed him, wetting his cheeks with her joyous tears.

After the initial glad reunion with his family, Anis proudly presented his wife and son. The welcome they gave Nell convinced her that all of the "tall tales" she had heard about the warmth and hospitality of Arabs were true. Many of the relatives could speak some English, which helped, but mostly it was the smiles and cordiality which made her feel a member of the large, gregarious Shorrosh family. Later she learned that among Arabs it was considered much status to have a blue-eyed American in a family.

From as far away as Amman the relatives gathered for the great coming home feast. In honor of Nell and Anis and little Salam they killed a lamb, dressed it, cut it in large chunks, cooked it in yogurt, and served it on a huge platter with mountains of rice covered with roasted pine nuts and almonds. Nell had been a little apprehensive about Arab food, but she found the *mansaf* dinner delicious.

After the meal the men gathered in the living room and the women in the sitting room. Even though Anis had told Nell about this custom, it still seemed strange to her. The real star of the occasion was Salam. Em Assad had fallen in love with him at first sight. And all the women billed and cooed over him, even though he had a cold and was running a bit of a fever.

The happy couple had a few days to spend with Em Assad before reporting to the hospital in Ajlun. Em Assad kept worrying about the little diaper shirts in which Salam was dressed. They exposed his tummy, which all Arab mothers knew meant he must be cold. Nell assured her that with the little booties on his feet, the baby was fine, in spite of a runny nose.

When Em Assad began complaining too much about the way her grandson was being taken care of, Anis took her aside and reassured her. "Mother, Nell is a graduate nurse. This may be her first child, but she does know what she is doing." There was no more interference, and Nell and Em Assad soon became real friends.

Anis left Nell with his mother and went ahead to check things out at the hospital. The trip down the bumpy, winding road to Ajlun brought back many memories. The sight of the Gilead Mountains was a real balm to his soul. Soon he was climbing the steep hill to the Baptist hospital. He was welcomed by the staff, and shown to the little green "gate house" that was part of the wall around the compound where he and his family would live. Dr. John Roper, a new addition to the staff since Anis had left for the States, showed him through the house. It had two large rooms, a smaller room, a kitchen, and a bathroom with a real tub.

"Nell will be very pleased," Anis exclaimed. "I'm sure she didn't expect real plumbing this far out in the country."

Before leaving, Anis took time to walk through the old, familiar hospital building. He went down into the basement where he found the same washerwomen working, just as he had left them nearly six years before. They greeted him with wide smiles, so pleased that he had not forgotten them.

But as he drove away he couldn't help but be humbled by comparing his life with theirs. All that he had done in the past years, the places he had visited, the friends he had made, the honors that had come his way. And all that time they were squatting on those same low stools, scrubbing their lives away on the hospital linen. He had to whisper a heartfelt "thank you" for the many opportunities he had been given.

He was driving along, singing loudly, enjoying himself, when he came upon a sight that chilled his blood. Off to his right, in a low, flat valley, was a D.P. camp. He felt compelled to turn aside and investigate. He drove to the outskirts, and parked his car, and got out to walk around and talk to some of the people.

He found that the little tents erected for the first Palestinian *lajieen* had been replaced by more permanent hovels, each smaller than a one-car garage. They had been built by the U.N., adjoining one another, row upon row, for about $100 each. In these tiny windowless huts lived nearly 80,000 people. Six, eight, ten and often more to a dwelling, with one water spigot for every five families and no sewerage. He was told that there were still a million refugees living in such camps.

The hopelessness he saw in their sad eyes and the underlying bitterness which he sensed among these people who had lived as refugees for over a decade was heartbreaking. The injustice of it all overwhelmed him. He was so grateful for his uncles who had kept his family from a similar fate. Those with relatives to help, or marketable skills had been assimilated into the mainstream of Jordan, Syria, Lebanon, and other Arab countries. But what good is a farmer without a farm? Or a shepherd without his sheep?

Poor, rocky Jordan had had enough trouble providing for its own one million population before being inundated with another million homeless, helpless *lajieen*, who owned only what they could carry on their backs. It was so unfair. And the United Nations continued to go through the annual travesty of reaffirming the resolution that would permit these people to return to their homes, or at least compensate them for their losses.

What made this condition seem all the sadder was the knowledge that most people in America had forgotten they even existed. Anis wondered how much longer his Palestinian brothers and sisters would continue to rot away in such a futile existence before rebellion and terrorism would break out. Surely it was inevitable that the generation that was being born and bred in such an unjust captivity would someday explode in violence.

He continued on to Irbid with the compelling thought etched in his brain, *God spared me from such a life for a purpose. I must fulfill that purpose and make my life count for Him.*

Nell (second from right) with hospital nurses at the Ajlun Baptist Hospital in Jordan, 1959. Crusader castle ruins are in the background.

Nell and Salam in Ajlun, Jordan, 1960.

Anis, Nell, Salam, Paul, and Em Assad (Anis' mother) at At-Tayyibah, Jordan, 1961.

King Hussein of Jordan (center, in uniform) with admirers at the Ajlun Baptist Hospital, including Anis (front center), 1960.

12

THE MINISTRY

They moved into the gatehouse and began work. Anis was to serve as the hospital chaplain, preach in neighboring churches, teach a Bible class in the boys' school, and serve as a village evangelist. Nell was given a few days to set up housekeeping before she was expected to begin teaching in the nursing school.

Nell found adjusting to the culture easier in some ways then anticipated. The Arab women were more modest than their American counterparts, but they seemed to feel that since her dresses reached below the knee they were acceptable. Of course she always wore sleeves. But she found it impossible to get used to wearing a scarf to church, and compromised by wearing a small pillbox-type hat on Sunday mornings. She continued wearing her hair short, for it was more convenient for her nursing duties and no one complained about that breach of custom.

Her first big clash came with a telephone company man who came to install a phone in their home. He didn't want to put the phone where she wanted it. She only knew a few words of Arabic, but had learned to say "No." And she was very definite about where she wanted that phone. To her surprise and aggravation, he insisted on putting it across the room from where she told him. She stood in his way and refused to permit him to install the phone on the far side of the largest room of the house. That would make it too far from the bedroom and kitchen. Just as stubbornly, he refused to install it where she wanted, and indignantly left without hooking up the phone at all.

Anis returned home a short time later and Nell complained to him about the man's rudeness and how she had asserted her independence. "You mean you bossed a man around like that?" Anis demanded, aghast at her impudence.

"Well, of course I did," Nell asserted self-righteously. "After all . . . "

Anis didn't wait to hear her explanation. He dashed to the car and zoomed down the hill trying desperately to catch up with the irate telephone man. He caught up with him halfway to town, and one look at him showed the walk hadn't cooled down his temper one bit.

Anis offered him a ride, then after the installer was in the car explained to him that his wife was new to the country and didn't yet understand the customs of the Middle East. The telephone man was determined to lodge an official complaint against the upstart woman who had dared order him around.

It took all the powers of persuasion Anis could muster to convince the offended man not to report her to the police. "But from now on," the man warned, "you had better keep your wife under control!"

Nell promised not to have any more run-ins with the telephone company. She was working hard trying to learn Arabic, but found it difficult because so many Arabs were trying to learn English and always wanted to practice on her. Anis was usually happy to help her, but sometimes became a little impatient if he thought she didn't catch on fast enough. Once when she asked how to say "sweater," he replied, "But I told you that just last week."

"Last week!" she exploded, hands on hips. "Do you have any idea how many words I've tried to learn since last week?"

But she was learning, and Anis was particularly pleased to see her making friends with Arab women as well as with the missionaries. Em Assad came and stayed with them for weeks at a time and taught Nell how to cook many Arabian dishes. Anis enjoyed seeing the two women in his life becoming so companionable.

Nell learned to make yogurt, the staple of many Arabian dishes. She would bring the milk to just the right temperature, add starter, then let it sit overnight covered in a blanket. She could also drain the water from it and make the spreadable white *lebani* cheese that Anis enjoyed so much. The first time she made *malfoof,* a concoction of stuffed, rolled cabbage leaves, he felt he now had the best of both worlds. A beautiful, companionable American wife, who could cook like an Arab.

Anis' years of self-discipline while studying in the States paid off well. For he habitually made efficient use of his time. In fact, he sometimes became a little restless because he felt he could be doing more. He often spoke at the early morning chapel services, then would witness in the wards, teach his Bible class, and then speak to those sitting in the waiting room of the outpatient clinic. He would still have energy to make trips to nearby towns to preach in the evenings.

Many of the local pastors began coming to him for counseling, encouragement, and advice. He was greatly relieved to find his years of schooling abroad had not created a breach with the national pastors. Perhaps the fact that he had been given the same status was a blessing in disguise, for as peers they were better able to communicate.

Other advantages to not being an officially appointed missionary were that he did not have to fill out all the forms or be on any of the required committees. He was flabbergasted when he discovered there were more committees at the hospital than missionaries.

In November he and Nell made a trip to Jerusalem, taking several side excursions to see some of the famous sights that draw tourists from all over the world. Anis had the privilege of climbing into some of the caves where the Dead Sea scrolls had been found. They also had the rare experience of seeing King Hussein of Jordan and the Shah of Iran riding together from Jerusalem to Jericho in a new Cadillac.

As Christmas approached Nell felt they should have a Christmas tree, just for Salam, of course. She wouldn't admit to being the least bit homesick. Anis explained how very precious trees are in Jordan, and the government didn't allow people to cut down trees just to decorate and then discard. She acquiesced, but he could tell from her expression that she was disappointed. He went to the authorities and got permission to cut a branch from a pine tree. They decorated it with bits of ribbon, cotton balls, and colored paper, made themselves a fine substitute tree, and enjoyed their first Jordanian Christmas.

The mission employees and their families enjoyed a turkey dinner, and afterward a Christmas play and a carol sing. But the very best present for Anis was the trip to Amman to see some of his relatives who had been allowed to cross the border into Jordan for a once-a-year 36-hour visit.

Anis had not seen many of the cousins since he was a boy, and he did not even recognize them at first. But there was one visitor who had not changed. His beloved grandmother had made the trip to see him and his wife and her new great-grandson. This was a reunion Anis had come to believe would never take place, but he was pleased to find the elderly widow as spry and winsome as ever. It was so good to see her after nearly 12 years, but the reunion rekindled his longing to walk once again through the streets of Nazareth and to return to the scenes of his childhood.

After New Year's Anis set up an office to counsel privately with persons who had heard him speak in the hospital. He also began a follow-up system for new believers and started a monthly conference with missionary Bill Hern for pastors and workers. He and Dr. Kamal Mansour, an Egyptian doctor who was now on the staff of the hospital, planned a weekly meeting for the young people. In addition he traveled throughout Jordan during February teaching the first Baptist study courses ever offered in the country.

Everywhere he preached and taught, God's Spirit seemed to be moving. There were converts in all the places he spoke, especially among the young people. And more opportunities to share his faith were constantly opening.

One day he was getting his shoes shined and the shoeshine man looked up at him and asked, "Haven't I seen you somewhere before?"

"It's possible," Anis answered. "I work at the Baptist Hospital in Ajlun."

"Ah, yes, I remember you. It was a little more than six years ago. I had a very serious operation and was close to death. Your Dr. Brown stayed with me. His Arabic wasn't too good, but I could tell he was genuinely concerned about me. That night he pulled a mattress into the ward and slept on the floor next to me. I never really understood what made him care so much for such a poor man as I."

It was a perfect opening for Anis to explain the love of God that changes men's hearts and gives them a concern for others. Because of his fluency in Arabic there were many such opportunities for Anis to reap the harvest of the seeds the missionaries had sown over the years.

In the spring Anis and Nell joined a group that set out in two large busses from Ajlun and Irbid for the long round trip to Jerusalem. Billy Graham was going to preach in the largest evangelical church in Old Jerusalem. After the services they felt very honored to be invited to eat dinner at the fanciest restaurant in town with the evangelist and his associate Grady Wilson.

During the meal, Dr. Graham asked Anis what he thought was the key to winning the Muslim world for Christ. "First, the Christians must really be Christians," he answered. "Till true believers show a difference in their lives the Muslims feel their religion is as good as ours. The problem is too many people are Christian by tradition only and have never had a saving experience with Jesus Christ."

In all his preaching Anis emphasized this need of recognizing the difference between religion and salvation. As more and more "traditional" Christians came to know God through personal experience, the churches became more alive and aggressive in their evangelism.

As the work was growing, so was Salam. By his first birthday, he was walking well and talking constantly, even though no one could understand what language he spoke. His mother was continuing to improve in Arabic and could carry on a conversation by this time. More significantly, she was expecting the arrival of a second child at the end of the year.

Summer Vacation Bible Schools in nearby towns increased Anis' already heavy work load. But he never complained about the added responsibilities. What did distress him were practices he felt had been engendered by some of the American missionaries.

It appeared to Anis that the missionaries held too much power and prominence. There were no national teachers in the new Baptist seminary in Beirut, where Arab preachers were trained. Missionaries did all the teaching, speaking through interpreters. Never would a national be allowed on the numerous missionary committees which dealt with the work. But what irritated Anis the most was the seating arrangements during chapel services at the Ajlun hospital. It seemed like such a small thing, and yet he felt it was very revealing, for the missionaries always sat in the front seats, then the national nurses and medical personnel, behind them the students, and finally the laborers, and, if they were invited, the washerwomen. He couldn't help but wonder if Jesus would have arranged them differently. And hadn't they read the New Testament Book of James?

Perhaps he had thought that missionaries were superhuman, ultra saints who were to be perfect in all things, but in working with them daily he detected faults that were disillusioning.

One missionary in particular seemed always to be on Anis' back. Anis felt he was jealous, though it seemed hard to believe that any Christian, especially a missionary, could resent another preaching to larger crowds, winning more to Christ, having more influence, and being in closer fellowship with the national believers, but that seemed to be the problem.

At the same time, Anis had become conscious more than ever of his own need for a deeper spiritual life. He vowed to begin reading the Bible through each year on his knees, following a regimen of three chapters each day and four on Sundays. Every morning before rising, often before opening his eyes, he recited the 23rd psalm as an assurance of God's presence. Now, he and his long time friend Suliman Summour, Samir Swais, a new employee, and a couple of others began spending more time in prayer seeking more of God's power in their lives.

One night, while driving Suliman, Samir Swais, Salim, a male nurse, and Dr. Samir Soloman, a Jordanian doctor at the hospital, back from services in Irbid, a great consciousness of sins and shortcomings fell on Anis' heart. It was as if a physical burden were weighing on his shoulders, and he began trembling, then shaking so violently that he had to pull off to the side of the road.

Dr. Soloman said softly, "God is dealing with Anis. Let's just pray and wait quietly."

With his friends praying silently for him, Anis felt suddenly transported to another dimension. The Lord seemed to say to him, "Ask anything you will, and I will give you the desire of your heart."

The only thought that came was a Bible verse, "Walk before Me, and be thou perfect" (Gen. 17:1). This came over and over. It was the real desire of his heart.

When he opened his eyes, a cloud had filled the car; they all saw it. It soon lifted, and with it the burden that had weighed so heavily on him. Now he felt filled with peace and love. A calm, tranquil peace such as he had never known and an all-encompassing love for God.

Dr. Soloman asked if he should drive the rest of the way. Anis said, "No, thank you. The Lord is driving with us." It was after midnight when Anis slipped into his home.

Nell awoke and asked. "Who's with you?"

Anis looked around and saw no one. "Only Jesus is with me," he told her. "Don't be afraid."

The next day she noticed that he seemed to be living in a cloud, but didn't understand the significance of what had happened. He felt so completely enveloped in God's Spirit that he was living in a form of constant communication with his Saviour. All over the large compound people noticed a powerful presence. It seemed that every prayer he breathed was answered instantly. Every person to whom he witnessed was overcome by God's convicting Spirit.

The team went for a short visit to Amman, and while there some of the Christians asked Anis to go with them to visit a blind man on his deathbed. As Anis approached the bed, he felt compelled to pray for the man's healing. He knelt with the others around the dying man and asked that he be "raised up by the power of Jesus." The man recovered his sight immediately. His heart attack had also left him partially paralyzed. Before their eyes he sat up in his bed and in three days was normal again.

When they returned to the hospital, Anis was the speaker in the early morning chapel services that week. He tried to share with the hospital staff the joy he had felt in the Lord since his experience on the road from Irbid. He admonished them to forget past grievances, forgive each other, and to learn to love one another more, so that they might be a better witness to the people who came from over 200 towns and villages to the famed hospital.

Some of the missionaries were highly incensed, and felt he was out of line to dare suggest they might have a need for repentance and revival. A few gave him strong hints that he should calm down a little, and not get so carried away with his messages. But he could not disobey the inner voice which compelled him to speak the truth as he saw it.

The next morning he preached from Isaiah: "My well-beloved hath a vineyard in a very fruitful hill. And He fenced it, and gathered out the stones thereof, and planted it with the choicest vine, and built a tower in the midst of it, and also made a winepress therein; and He looked that it should bring forth grapes, and it brought forth wild grapes" (5:1-2).

Anis compared this to the hospital building that had been built on a steep hill, with a fence around it and planted with the choicest people to work there for Him. But he declared that if they brought forth "wild grapes"—literally "bad grapes" in the Arabic text—then the same judgment would fall on their work as on the vineyard that Isaiah wrote about. Their works would be "laid waste" unless they themselves were right with God.

Many on the staff felt it was the most powerful sermon they had ever heard. But the missionaries called an emergency meeting. Since the Lovegrens had been very close to the Shorroshs, they appointed Dr. Lovegren to go talk to Anis and warn him to tone down his messages.

Anis felt strongly that he must obey God, rather than man— even the missionaries for whom he had always had great love and respect. On the way to the chapel services the next morning he was stopped by the mission chairman, and warned, "This is your last chance to preach in the chapel."

"Well, if it is my last time, I am grateful to you for the opportunity." Then he preached the message he had been impressed to bring. He was certain it was his last sermon to that group.

After the services some of the missionaries asked Nell why she didn't try to calm Anis down. Their veiled hints that Anis was losing his mind became outright accusations. She was greatly distressed and reduced to tears at a time when she was seven months pregnant and not feeling well physically.

As an employee of the mission, Anis was under the direction of the missionaries. Some thought the best solution would be to assign him to a church away from the hospital. While they were considering this, Nell went into labor. The hospital staff rallied around to do all that was possible to insure a safe delivery. Beautiful little Deborah was born tiny but perfectly formed. She lived only a few minutes.

Nell was heartbroken; Anis, totally crushed. For two days he ate and drank nothing as he grieved for the infant daughter he never got to hold in his arms. When the tiny coffin was placed in a knoll under some tall pine trees, he questioned God's wisdom in allowing such a tragedy to happen. But even as he stood beside the grave the realization came that the tremendous spiritual experience he had been given was meant to prepare him to with-stand this sorrow. In His great love, God had fortified him that he might cope with this grievous loss.

The missionaries decided that the Shorroshes should move to At-Tayyibah, a town of about 5,000 population that had recently lost its resident medical doctor. At-Tayyibah was about 15 miles northwest of Ajlun, but a tortuous 35-mile drive through Irbid. It had a small church and school at the mission station, as well as the clinic. The missionary committee felt that Anis could pastor the church and supervise the school, and Nell could treat emergency medical cases and help the doctor who would make weekly visits to the clinic.

As soon as Nell was physically able, they began packing. Workers from the hospital helped pack and load their belongings into the beat-up old Ford and a truck. When they were unloading in At-Tayyibah, Anis found that one of the male nurses had written a Scripture verse on a box: Genesis 50:30. Anis looked it up and found it came from the story of Joseph and his brothers. It read, "But as for you, ye thought evil against me; but God meant it unto good." His friends were evidently trying to en-courage him that the move would prove to be beneficial for him.

Little did they know how prophetic they would be.

13

THE PREPARING

The two-story, ten-room house they moved into in At-Tayyibah had been built by a British doctor who believed in having nothing but the best. The workmanship in the cut rock house was an excellent example of the beautiful masonry work that abounds in Jordan. Having such a large, commodious house, and because Nell would have daily chores in the clinic as well as all day Thursdays, they invited Em Assad to live with them, for Samuel, Anis' younger brother, was now studying in the U.S.

Anis was exhilarated by a feeling of freedom. Perhaps it was the breadth of the sweeping view from their new home. From the upstairs window he could see Mt. Tabor rising in the west, and to the north, beyond groves of olive trees and fields of flowing wheat, stood majestic Mt. Hermon crowned with sparkling white snow. Or could it be he no longer felt someone was perpetually looking over his shoulder?

It is said that from At-Tayyibah one can see 20 villages on a clear day, and naturally Anis considered them all part of his parish. He liked being in charge, being his own boss. Yet with all the responsibilities he still felt a strange uneasiness. A feeling that he wasn't doing all the Lord wanted of him. He began writing an Arabic exposition of the Book of Ephesians and sending news reports back to Baptist papers in America.

As an employee of the Jordanian mission he still had to report to one of the missionaries once a month to discuss any problems. The small staff on the At-Tayyibah compound got along well and he really didn't have much to report, so usually they wound up talking about that missionary's troubles. Anis preferred to handle any staff difficulties by personal example rather than by giving orders.

When the sewerage system clogged up one time, Anis found the watchmen and the driver arguing about who would descend into the slimy pit to clear out the pipe. Each thought it beneath his dignity to do such disgusting manual labor.

"Well, since you gentlemen are above such menial tasks, I'll take care of it myself," Anis told the astonished employees.

Then he proceeded to remove the manhole cover, and despite the nauseating stench, lowered himself into the sewer. The workmen were shocked that he would do such a job and became very ashamed at their own unwillingness. Anis never had trouble with either of them again about any assignment.

Because water is scarce much of the year in Jordan, the cistern under the house caught the occasional rainwater to use for washing and bathing. The scarcity forced the Shorroshes to limit themselves to two baths a week. One evening after climbing out of the tub, and watching the water go down the drain, two-year-old Salam announced that he knew what made rain. "What's that, Son?" Anis asked him.

"Well, Jesus is up in heaven, and after He takes a bath, He pulls the plug and the water comes down for us."

That bit of wisdom got him a big laugh and a delighted hug from his adoring father. Salam was such a joy to the whole family that they were all praying anxiously that the new baby which was expected would be born safely.

Nell was becoming quite a proficient midwife. Since Arab women, and Muslims especially, prefer a woman to a male doctor to help with a delivery, her services were often called on. One night a frantic message was delivered by horseback that a woman had given birth, and was hemorrhaging badly. Nell got the telephone operator out of bed and called Dr. Lovegren in Ajlun. He said it was probably a retained placenta and told her what emergency procedure to follow. There was no time for him to get there.

A rough 10-minute drive over a dirt road brought Nell and Anis to the small home. The woman was lying on a mattress in a corner surrounded by a crowd of sorrowing relatives. Anis moved them out of the room as Nell quickly took her blood pressure. Her pulse was hardly discernible. She was sinking fast.

Anis tied the plasma bottle to a nail on the wall while Nell strained to insert the needle in a vein with only the light from a flickering kerosene lamp. For an agonizing 15 minutes Nell searched for the nearly invisible vein while Anis prayed earnestly. At last the life-giving fluid began flowing into the motionless form. While Nell and the practical nurse, Muntaha, prepared to remove the afterbirth, Anis went outside to inform the two dozen or more relatives of the progress being made. Salameh, their driver, had given out some gospels and tracts and Anis noticed one of the men straining to read the first words of the Gospel of John by flashlight. While Nell's training was being used to save a life, he was able to share the Good News of the new life available through Christ.

In July 1961 Anis performed his first baptismal service as five new believers were added to their membership. The following week the At-Tayyibah mission was organized into a Baptist church. Anis was thrilled about the success, but was still burdened for surrounding Muslim villages.

The only way to get to preach in a Muslim village was to travel with a medical doctor. Dr. Petros Baz, an Assyrian who had lived most of his life in Jordan, often went with Anis. They would go to the center of a village and say that a doctor was there. The people would gather for medical attention, and Anis would preach to them before they were permitted to see the doctor. He realized he had a kind of captive audience, but it was the only way some of them would ever hear the Gospel.

It was discouraging that when Muslims attended the church services, many of the Christians complained. They didn't want the Muslim boys looking at their girls. Some of the Arab Christians even believed that a Muslim could not be saved.

As the time neared for Nell's own delivery, Anis was rather anxious about the hour-and-a-half drive to Ajlun, now on paved roads. So when she announced one morning that she wasn't feeling just right, he insisted they leave immediately for the hospital. She saw no reason to hurry, but Anis insisted. They kissed Salam good-bye and left him contented in the hands of his grandmother.

They arrived at a crossroad only to find the road was blocked. "What's the matter?" Anis demanded of one of the soldiers.

"Road's closed today. King Hussein is coming," the soldier replied briskly.

Anis jumped from, the car and dashed over to the officer in charge. Nell sat calmly in the car watching as he made frantic gestures to the officer who just continued shaking his head. She was amused at how animated Anis was while indicating with his hands her extreme condition. Using all of his great powers of persuasion Anis finally convinced the man to let them cross.

When they got to Ajlun, Nell said there was no need for Anis to hang around. She could stay with the Lovegrens, and if anything exciting happened they would call him. He had hardly gotten down the hill when labor began in earnest. By the time he got back to At-Tayyibah the switchboard had closed down and they could not contact him, so he didn't learn till the next morning that he had a new son. Paul Anis. A handsome, healthy addition to the family, born on September 23, 1961.

Besides his regular pastoral duties, Anis was sometimes confronted with situations he had never been told about at seminary. One problem concerned an elderly couple. Because the old man was blind, the wife slept in the chicken coop to keep thieves from taking their precious fowls. This arrangement did not suit her husband. Anis solved the difficulty by giving them a wire box. They could now keep the chickens in the bedroom and resume sleeping together.

In a small town nearby two brothers had been quarreling for over two years. Since they were the only Christian families in the village, Anis thought it a very poor testimony to their Muslim neighbors, that Christians, especially family members could not resolve their differences. So it was with great personal satisfaction that he was able to fulfill his Arab name, Abu Salam, "father of peace," by healing the animosity that had existed between the brothers.

A problem the "father of peace" could not solve was the continuing animosity between Israel and the Arab countries. The passing of time had only heightened tensions. Frustrated and bitter young men from the depressing Palestinian refugee camps were making suicide raids into Israel. While he could not justify the raids—many of which were retaliatory for Israeli forays—he could understand the bitterness which the young *lajieen* felt. As he often told Nell, "What does the world expect of people who have no hope? But for the grace of God I would probably be joining them."

For its part, Israel kept up a "war of nerves," sending fighter planes in February 1962 to bomb the Suez Canal, which the Egyptians had again nationalized. The following month the Israelis made a lightning invasion of Syria, that took a heavy toll of life and caused widespread destruction. Then the Israelis withdrew, claiming that Syrian units had harassed their fishermen on the Sea of Galilee below the boundary. Syria succeeded in getting the U.N. to "condemn" Israel for following a policy of reprisals against Arab neighbors—even the U.S. and Britain voted for the censure—but the edgy peace continued to hang by a slim thread.

During all this tension Anis kept making the rounds of his "parish." One of his favorite companions was Abu Sayyeh, a refugee from across the Jordan. Abu Sayyeh was a mystical sort of fellow who sometimes surprised Anis with a prophecy.

One day they were driving home and discussing the new Arab believers in Old Jerusalem who were interested in forming a church.

"They will want you to become their pastor!" Abu Sayyeh announced. "Perhaps you will, but you will not remain long. God is going to send you around the world preaching for Him."

Anis laughed at the ridiculous idea.

He and Nell continued at the At-Tayyibah station. In August he initiated another first for Jordan, a church homecoming with "dinner on the grounds." He had enjoyed these annual rituals while a student in Mississippi, and felt the gregarious Arab Christians would like them also. The festival was a huge success. Dr. Lovegren came from Ajlun, representing the missionaries, along with the Reverend Jeryes Dalleh, the new Arab president of the Jordanian Baptist Convention, and the Reverend Hani Nasrallah, the pastor of the Irbid church. They all joined in the thanksgiving services for the tiny new At-Tayyibah church that had enjoyed a 62% increase in membership during the past year. This involved only eight new members, but they were gratful for each one. There were still only about 100 Baptists in all of Jordan at this time.

By this time Nell had become a veteran obstetrician. Because her last three deliveries had been boys, the people were saying, "Her hands are blessed." Her own boys were growing rapidly.

Salam spoke both Arabic and English, and Paul was jabbering away in an incomprehensible combination of both.

As January 1963 approached, the Shorroshes were beginning to think of a leave of absence. Had they been Board "appointees," they would have been eligible for a year's furlough with continuation of salaries and paid transportation to the States.

The Jordan Baptist Mission agreed to pay travel expenses for Nell, but Anis would have to raise his own. "Lord, if You want me to go, lay it on someone's heart to provide," Anis prayed. An offer came from the Weller Avenue Baptist Church of Baton Rouge, Louisiana to pay his fare.

With these provisions, they began making plans. Anis would enroll for graduate studies at New Orleans Seminary. They would spend time with Nell's family and visit friends and churches across the country. It was so exciting they could hardly wait.

Before leaving the Middle East, they went to Egypt, where Anis participated in a church stewardship conference in Cairo. Then they flew north to Beirut for the first graduation exercises of the Arab Baptist Seminary. When they finally boarded their flight for the States, Anis again felt a deep thankfulness for all the opportunities which the Lord had opened. Yet he sensed that all these experiences were part of a larger plan for which the Lord was preparing him.

It was good to be back in the "Land of Plenty," as Anis termed America. Calls to speak came from the moment their plane landed. But first they visited relatives and friends and showed off their most prized possessions, Salam and Paul. Not till they had settled in an apartment on the seminary campus in New Orleans and Anis had enrolled as a special student did he begin again the weekend safaris which had been so much a part of his earlier years in the U.S.

Anis was in Mobile for a revival when their third child decided to make his appearance. Dr. and Mrs. A. L. Lovegren, the parents of their missionary friends in Jordan, drove Nell to the Baptist hospital and then called Anis. There were no planes available that night so after speaking Anis got Nell's brother-in-law, Louis Reynolds, to drive him back to New Orleans to be with Nell.

He arrived at 2 A.M. Steven Anis appeared two hours later, and with much regret, Anis took a 6 A.M. bus back to Mobile to fulfill his commitment there. It was a rather hectic experience for both parents, but Anis promised to be there in style to bring Nell and Steven home from the hospital.

When he returned from Mobile, Anis headed for a used car lot to find a replacement for their old Ford which they had sold back in Jordan. It hadn't been worth the freight expense of a second trip across the ocean. With a rapidly growing family, he decided to look for a station wagon. The car salesman assured him he had "just the thing."

He led Anis over to a gleaming wagon, raised the hood, and said, "Listen to this motor purr." Then leaving his customer, he got in the car and flipped on the ignition. Somehow the car slipped into first and jumped forward, jamming Anis between two car bumpers. When Anis screamed in pain, the salesman slammed the car into reverse. Anis fell to the ground and lay writhing in pain on the sea shells that are substitutes for gravel in New Orleans.

Mercifully, an ambulance came in a few minutes and rushed him to the hospital. Sedatives dulled the pain and he was wheeled in for X rays. When the pictures showed no broken bones, Anis called and asked the senior Lovegrens if they would play Good Samaritan again.

On the way back to the campus the pain became so bad that Anis fainted. He revived briefly, then while being helped into the house fainted again. The Lovegrens found a student to spend the night with him and arranged for the boys to remain at the baby-sitter's.

It was the most pain-wracked episode of his life. All night long he screamed in agony. The next morning a bone specialist discovered a blood clot in his left leg. The doctor put him on medication and instructed, "Stay in bed." But when Nell and his new son were brought home, he got up and wobbled to the door on crutches to greet them.

The accident cost him a quarter of schooling. But in trying to make amends for the accident, the auto agency sold him a used wagon in excellent condition for $1,800. Anis put it to good use, traveling throughout the South and speaking in churches over 300 times, plus appearing at the mammoth Southern Baptist Convention in Atlantic City, New Jersey.

Shortly after the Convention a letter came from Jerusalem. The Arab believers had just formed the First Baptist Church there. Their first official act as a church had been to call Anis Shorrosh as their pastor.

Two missionaries who recently arrived home on furlough told him that the Arab work was at a critical stage, and he was needed. The Foreign Mission Board added its endorsement by offering to pay passage back.

Anis was flattered by the invitation and excited over the prospect of living in the most venerated city in Christendom. But he had hoped to work cn a doctorate in theology and was even offered free tuition and housing.

"Lord, give me assurance that I should go," he prayed. The conviction came that Jerusalem should be the next destination in his journey of discipleship.

14
THE COVENANT

Jerusalem in 1964. Golden Jerusalem. Sacred city of shrines and relics, churches and temples and mosques, droning prayers and plaintive dirges, and never-ending streams of pilgrims.

A city divided between Jordan and Israel, symbolic of the cleavage between Arabs and Jews which continued to threaten the peace of the world. Separated not only by the barbed wire that surrounded no-man's-land, but by hate, bitterness, and distrust.

A city of challenge for Anis and Nell.

Their first task was to find housing, which in the overcrowded "city of peace" was no simple thing. Finally they were able to rent a two-bedroom bungalow in suburban Beit Hanina, on the road to Ramallah. It was in a nice section populated by United Nations officials and friendly Muslims.

The Jerusalem Baptist Church in the Jordanian sector met in a basement room of a building near King Herod's Gate. The Baptist Book Store was upstairs and did a thriving business among pilgrims. The rent for both operations was paid by the Baptist Mission.

Although the new church had only 18 members, from 60 to 100 crowded into the basement auditorium to hear the new pastor. Services were held in both Arabic and English for the needs of the cosmopolitan population and the wide variety of international visitors.

At the first church business meeting after the new pastor's

arrival, they discussed whether to keep the Shorroshes' station wagon or sell it. The car was on the way but duty would cost $1,500, a sum which the members felt was beyond their means. As it was, the mission was having to pay half of Anis' monthly salary.

Anis felt the car was needed. His family had been unable to find housing in the city, and required transportation. Also, he said, he could carry numbers of people to meetings, and if necessary haul supplies. He gathered the men to pray about the problem.

"Lord, You know my heart," Anis prayed, "and You know I don't want a car if it isn't Your will. I don't have $1,500, but if You want me to have the car here to use in the work, give us a sign. Provide the money that we may know we have Your blessings in this matter."

A few days later a letter came from a lawyer in New Orleans. Anis was to receive $2,500 as a settlement for the injury to his legs that he had suffered in the car lot. This would more than cover the cost of customs, license, and freight charges on the car. It seemed a rather strange way of providing, but Anis thanked the Lord for the accident, and gladly accepted the money as from Him.

The purpose in providing the car was soon revealed as mission churches were opened in Ramallah, about 10 miles to the north, and Ma'daba across the Jordan River to the east. It would have been impossible for Anis to serve in all these places if he had not had private transportation.

Even with help from American friends, Anis' salary was not enough to pay their living expenses, so Nell enrolled Salam in kindergarten and obtained part-time nursing work with an obstetrician. Em Assad again came to live with them and cared for the two younger boys while Nell was at work.

Both Nell and Anis enjoyed being back among Arab believers. They were so enthusiastic and warm, and such eager listeners to Anis' sermons. And they sang so lustily and with such beautiful rhythm to the accompaniment of the piano as Nell played.

In Jerusalem, Anis was more in the main current of the Arab Christian world than he had been at At-Tayyibah. He began receiving invitations to speak from all over the Middle East. In November he was a part of an evangelistic team that held crusades in Lebanon and saw 600 make public decisions for Christ. Back in Jerusalem he held another successful revival that climaxed with a baptismal service in the River Jordan.

With the coming of cold weather Anis bought a Coleman kerosene heater for their home. It was still necessary to wear warm clothing in the house for the hard, marblelike cement block floors were always cold, and the heat did not circulate well.

They made friends with a Muslim family that lived across the street from them. The middle-aged gentleman and his two wives were most amicable and they visited back and forth. As was the custom, the Muslim neighbors always visited them on Christian holidays and the Shorroshes would reciprocate on Muslim holy days.

The two wives came to visit Nell and Em Assad one day. While drinking the traditional thick, black Arabian coffee, the large, pleasant-faced older one remarked to Nell, "You are always rushing around so."

"Yes," her younger counterpart agreed, "you go to meetings, you hurry to work, you run after your children. And still you must keep your house clean and make the meals. You have no time for leisure."

"Well, I do keep busy all right," Nell agreed with a little giggle. "But I really don't mind; it keeps life interesting."

"We have a solution for you," the first wife informed her seriously. She glanced at the second wife, who being rather timid, shook her head, motioning for the number one wife to continue.

"What you should do," the older woman continued, "is have your husband marry another wife. She can do the housework and leave you free for all the goings and comings."

Nell almost choked. She didn't want to hurt the dear women's feelings, but not laughing made her want to laugh all the more. She glanced at Em Assad who was having difficulty containing herself also.

"I'm afraid that would never work," Nell finally thought to say. "You see my husband has enough trouble with just me. I don't think he could manage with two wives."

As if to prove how busy life was for the Shorroshes, 21 relatives descended on them to spend Christmas. They borrowed 10 mattresses from different neighbors and for four nights slept people all over the house, even in the hallways.

But despite the visit from Anis' relatives the Christmas season seemed very different in Jerusalem. Since only a minority of the population of the city were Christians, there was not much holiday spirit around. Then too this was the glad/sad time of year when loved ones living in "Occupied Palestine" were allowed a short visit with relatives.

The new year of 1965 found Anis busily completing the Arabic commentary on Ephesians he had worked on so long and so diligently. The Owen Gregorys, friends in Mississippi, were paying for the printing. The 186-page book was titled, *The Glory of Christ in the Church* and was received with great enthusiasm by the Arabic-speaking pastors, whose libraries in their native tongue were so limited.

Invitations for Anis to hold revivals kept coming in from Egypt, Syria, Lebanon, and other countries, but mission policy permitted him to be away from the church only three Sundays for extra preaching and two for vacation which he also used for revivals. Anis argued that the church had a number of excellent lay preachers who could free him to do more, but the missionaries said the rule must stand.

He was asked frequently why, with his education, he wasn't teaching in the Arab Baptist Seminary in Beirut. His stock reply was that policy called for only missionary teachers, even though half or most teaching sessions were devoted to translation of English lectures into Arabic. "We don't make the rules," he would frequently say. "The Foreign Mission Board feels that the missionaries should teach, since Baptist mission money goes to operate the institutions."

When summer came, Anis could report to supporters back in the States that the church in Jerusalem had doubled in membership during its first year. "We have a truly international fellowship," he wrote. "Our members include Greek, Scottish, Canadian, American, Lebanese, Jordanian, and Armenian Christians. Additionally, numbers of tourist pilgrims attend our services and leave the Holy Land with a renewed zeal to live for Christ."

And, lest life should become boring, there were little incidents like the morning when Sameer Wakim, one of the new believers in the church, came banging on their door.

"My wife is in labor," he announced. "I need to borrow your car to get her to the hospital."

"Sure, Man," Anis replied, handing him the keys, "and maybe you'd better take my wife along, just in case."

"Well, they tell me first babies usually take their time, but it might be wise to have a midwife along," he agreed.

The wisdom of that decision was soon proved as Sameer flew along the highway to the Baptist Hospital in Ajlun while his wife's pains were coming closer and closer. They were about half way there when Nell realized they weren't going to make it. She arranged a makeshift bed in the back of the station wagon, and 15 minutes short of the hospital her "blessed hands" delivered a healthy, yowling baby boy. Lacking facilities and instruments, she tore the end from her cotton slip to tie the cord.

The doctors at the hospital proclaimed both mother and son in fine condition, but the father and Nell were total wrecks.

In the fall Anis instigated another first for Jordanian Baptists, "An Hour with Sacred Music." The basement chapel was filled to capacity. Nell played, the Doctors Roper, husband and wife medical team, came from Ajlun to sing and a small choir from the Girls' Blind School sang in both Arabic and English. Then Anis sang a solo, his own translation of "How Great Thou Art."

The concert celebrated the gift of a secondhand baby grand Baldwin piano to the church by the mission. The concert was so successful, and the people enjoyed it so much, the church voted to make it an annual affair.

During the Christmas holidays that year one of the members of the church, Antone Salah, had an unusual experience. While visiting a friend of his family's he met her younger sister Samia, who had crossed over from Israel to visit during the time that was allowed. Antone took one look at this petite young lady with doe-like brown eyes, fair complexion, a pleasing smile, and knew she was the one for him.

As soon as he could break Samia away from her sister, Antone maneuvered her aside and broke all custom by asking if she would stay in Jerusalem and become engaged to him. Samia blushed, hesitated, and then declared "I must return home this evening."

Antone kept pleading for her to stay.

"No, I cannot," she said gently, trying not to hurt his feelings. "My parents are quite old, and if I did stay past the time, the border guards would never permit me back to see them again.

I would at least have to return to tell them good-bye and get my clothes."

"If you should decide you would like to, we could go this afternoon and purchase your rings to settle the engagement. Then we could be married immediately upon your return."

This was quite a decision to have to make on such short notice, but Samia inquired of her sister and was told that Antone was a fine respectable young man of excellent reputation. In a dreamlike haze she accepted his proposal.

While Samia was back in Israel, Antone called on Anis to help make all the arrangements, since there was no mail service between the two countries. Anis agreed to perform the ceremony and Nell was to play the piano. Since Christmastime was past, no relatives would be allowed to cross over for the wedding, so they invited all the church members to help make it a happy occasion.

The wedding day was a sad one for Samia's parents. As an Arab living in Israel Samia was free to leave the country anytime she chose, but by leaving other than at the stipulated times during holidays, she would never be allowed back in again. In accordance with Arab custom she dressed in her wedding gown and left her parents to go to her new husband. It was a tearful farewell.

Anis had dropped Nell off, all dressed up for the occasion, at the beauty parlor to have her hair done. Then he and his mother went to the church to make sure everything was set up and to help greet the guests. When the time came to pick Nell up, Anis was busy talking to people, so he sent a cab for her.

This was Anis' first wedding ceremony, and he was as nervous as the groom. He had even chosen to wear a clerical collar for the auspicious occasion. All the guests were soon assembled, but no Nell. Antone was fidgeting, but no Nell. The bride was waiting, but no one was there to provide music.

Finally they began without the music. Anis had sent the cab long before and couldn't imagine what had happened to Nell, for she had been so anxious to attend this wedding. The vows were exchanged, the groom gave his lovely bride a kiss, and everyone left for the reception which was to be held at Antone's parents' house.

Anis drove by the beauty shop in case Nell was still there. She was—and fuming. Absolutely furious after waiting for so long a time to be picked up, she climbed in the car, vowing, "I'll never forget this as long as I live!" and dissolved into a torrent of frustrated tears.

Anis tried to explain but his words were not heard. "Honey, I sent a cab long ago. Maybe he lost the address. Or maybe he asked for you by your American name and the beauty shop knew you only as Em Salam. Or . . . whatever happened, I'm sorry." His voice trailed off as he saw it was no use. He would just have to wait until she calmed down.

He went on to the reception, but she remained outside in the car, pouting. Happily the newlyweds began their marriage in a more pleasant mood. Although Nell kept her vow never to "forget," she did soon forgive.

Samia, the new bride, had come from a Greek Orthodox family, and found the Baptists quite different from what she was used to. For one thing her new husband was always going to church. She had been raised to go on Easter and at Christmas, and for special occasions like weddings and christenings, but Antone went every single Sunday and Wednesday night, too. He never insisted that she accompany him, but after awhile she became curious about what went on at the church that had captured her husband's total devotion.

When she asked to go with him, naturally, he was thrilled. She found the informal, friendly services totally different from what she had been accustomed to, and was delighted by the difference. She enjoyed the music and entered into the hymn singing.

When Anis got up to preach she listened intently. His sermon was totally new to her. Not only was it understandable, but it was interesting. She was captivated. It seemed strange, but she felt that "Brother Anis" really believed everything he was saying. That he felt this was the most important message in the world. The idea that God really loved her, and cared for her as an individual enough to die for her sins.

This accounted for the difference in her husband's life. She realized the need for change in her life, but it took a few weeks before she received Christ as her personal Saviour. Two months later Anis had the joy of baptizing her in the River Jordan.

More and more converts were being baptized. Sunday School attendance was up to 85 at Ramallah and the people there were eager to organize their own church. But Anis was restless. He felt

God wanted him to widen his ministry, but he was bound under the restrictions of the mission.

He thought the solution might be a part-time job outside that would provide the income he had been receiving from the mission. Then he would be free. The church voted its approval and he began making inquiries. First he guided Baptist tour groups on a free-will offering basis for a week and earned more than the church paid him for a month. Then someone suggested radio broadcasting. He went to Radio Jerusalem and was tested in both British and American accents. The station offered to hire him immediately either full or part time.

To make the pressure greater, Nell was under great strain in her duties as head nurse at an obstetrical clinic that demanded not only full time but overtime as well. Then too she had to keep up with her family responsibilities. Em Assad had gone to stay with her eldest son and the boys needed a full-time mother.

The church had planned an outing at Emmaus on Friday of that same week. After the picnic Anis rolled out a rug he had brought along and lay down to enjoy the soft breeze that rustled through the pines overhead.

It was a low point in Anis' life. He lay moody and silent, wondering what to do. He felt torn in so many directions. Finally he looked up into the sky and asked, "Lord, what do You want me to do now? If You don't tell me, I think I'll go crazy."

A Voice as distinct as the One that had spoken to the two disciples so long before on the road to Emmaus from Jerusalem seemed to say, "Open and read." Anis pulled the little New Testament with Psalms from his shirt pocket and let it fall open. The first verse he saw when he looked down was Psalm 24:1: "The earth is the Lord's and the fulness thereof; the world, and they that dwell therein."

The message hit him hard: "See now, here you are worrying about how you will take care of your family if you go into full-time evangelism. You rush about, seeking jobs, putting your wife to work. That is not depending on Me. You are depending on your education, your training, your mission board, and the church, even on your wife.

"Can't you see that I own the whole world and everything in it? Surely it would be a small matter for Me to provide for your family. Each morning you say the words of the 23rd Psalm, but you don't really mean them. This day I shall make a covenant with you. If you will truly make Me your Shepherd, from this day forward I'll see that you want for nothing."

Warm tears covered Anis' face as he told the Lord, "I am sorry, forgive me. From this day forward I'll follow only You."

He was anxious to share the experience with Nell. He wasn't certain how she would react, but as soon as possible he got her alone in their room and explained what had happened.

"If that's what the Lord wants, I'm with you, Anis," she responded. He had never heard sweeter words. They knelt by the bed and dedicated themselves and their children anew to the Lord.

"This will be a real venture in faith," Anis warned afterward. "I'll be without a regular income."

Nell smiled. "Well, then, let's really depend on Him. I'll quit my job, too. If you are to be free to travel and preach as the Lord opens doors, then I'll need to be at home with the boys."

Anis gave his resignation to the church that Sunday in July 1966. "Long ago I completed the three years of service I promised for my scholarship," he added. "So I am breaking no agreement.

"Nor am I angry with any of you or any missionary. I may disagree with some of the rules, but I will continue to appreciate all that the missionaries have done for me. I hope we can all continue in good fellowship."

Tears flowed freely as many begged Anis to reconsider, but there was no changing his mind.

Nell also quit her job. When word got around of what they had done, many people, including some of the missionaries, thought they had acted very hastily and unwisely. Stories spread that Anis was going to establish his own church, along with other rumors of what he planned to do. Anis and Nell tried to squelch the loose talk, explaining that they didn't want to take anyone away from the church. It was just that they both felt the Lord wanted Anis in full-time evangelism.

Now they would see what would happen.

15

THE EVANGELIST

The news spread rapidly that Anis Shorrosh had entered full-time evangelism. So often before he had felt frustrated and fettered. Now he could witness wherever the Lord led.

During the first few days he teamed with a close friend, the youthful Jan Willem van der Hoeven, later to become the keeper of the Garden Tomb. They presented the Gospel at the Friends' Meeting Hall, the Anglican and Lutheran churches, and twice at the Catholic Fellowship Hall in Bethlehem. Anis appeared alone at the Helen Keller Home, the Orthodox Club near the Church of the Nativity, and at the Evangelical home and the Greek Orthodox Seminary in Ramallah. And he showed evangelical films at the Pauline Seminary in Beit Hanina. In three weeks he spoke to over 1,250 people who would never have come to the little Baptist church. "Surely God is good," he rejoiced to Nell. "And there is no greater joy than being in His will."

He and van der Hoeven decided to go on a preaching tour. They would travel wherever the Lord would lead, preach as they found opportunity, eat if food was provided, and fast if not. They just felt an overpowering urge to share the Gospel. Immediately.

Itinerating through Jordan, Syria, and Lebanon, the blond, blue-eyed Dutchman and the dark Arab made such contrasting appearances, yet they were so obviously one in the Spirit. Jan Willem preached and Anis interpreted, but the Lord anointed them in a special way so it seemed not two but one voice speaking in harmony. They held services in Baptist, Christian and Missionary

Alliance, Catholic, and Greek Orthodox churches, and anywhere else they could get a hearing. They even held one service in a huge old Crusader castle. The largest crowd was in a Catholic church where the people sat with rapt attention as if they had never heard of a personal experience with Christ.

Along the way they met a squad of international youth from Operation Mobilization. They joined forces, with the young people giving out literature and singing before Anis and van der Hoeven preached.

One night the Dutchman didn't know what he was supposed to preach about. He had prayed and prayed, and nothing came. All the assurance he had was that when he rose to speak it would be revealed to him. He stood up before the crowd and let his Bible fall open. Anis, who was interpreting, did the same. They looked down and were startled to see that both Bibles had fallen open to the same passage. It seemed clear this was the message the Lord had chosen for that night.

Perhaps the highlight of the summer came in the town of Ma'daba, in southern Jordan, just a few miles from Mt. Nebo where Moses stood to survey the Promised Land. The cobwebs in the church seemed a symbol of the inactivity of the professing Christians. Then during the service, apathy changed to hostility when some of the people started hissing at the speaker. The hissing spread across the audience till it seemed the building was permeated with animosity.

Anis' eyes flashed and he shouted something in Arabic which his Dutch partner didn't understand. But the noise stopped and everyone suddenly became attentive. Later van der Hoeven asked Anis what he had said. "I just told them, 'Shut your mouths, in the name of Jesus,' " Anis replied. "I didn't really intend to say it. It just came out."

The next day the evangelists and the Operation Mobilization youth climbed Mt. Nebo. There they fasted and prayed for God to demonstrate His power in Ma'daba. They claimed the town in the name of Jesus.

Toward the end of the services that night one young man could not wait for the invitation to receive Christ. He ran forward and fell on his knees, weeping aloud for God's mercy. While he was praying another came forward. Then another and another. The revival broke loose before the sermon had been concluded. And before the week was over all of Ma'daba had witnessed the power of God.

At the end of summer Anis and van der Hoeven returned to Jerusalem praising God for all the victories. By this time Nell and Anis were in bad financial straits. They tried to sell their station wagon to the Baptist Mission and had begun selling furniture piece by piece when Anis received another message from the Lord. "Wait a minute," the Lord seemed to be saying. "That's not the way to depend on Me. I didn't need Isaac as a sacrifice, I just wanted to get to Abraham through Isaac. I don't need you to sell your possessions—I just want you to depend on Me."

"OK, Lord," Anis responded. "My life is in Your hands."

Anis received an invitation to represent Jordan at the first World Evangelism Congress which was to be held in Berlin. The invitation included a round trip ticket. Em Assad had returned so Nell wouldn't be alone with the boys. Anis felt the provision providential and took off for 10 days in Germany.

After checking into his hotel Anis found a note in his mailbox asking him to come to Billy Graham's room for prayer. They had a happy time together.

Later, Dr. Graham was to introduce Anis to the Congress. Before the time came, Anis was given a form on which he was to list degrees earned, books written, and any other great accomplishments. Anis handed the paper to Dr. Graham, but before the evangelist stood up, Anis said, "Forget all this stuff and just let me read the Scriptures."

"We have with us a young man who has had a marvelous experience with the Lord," Dr. Graham said. "His name is Anis Shorrosh, and he comes to us from Jerusalem." Anis considered the introduction the best he had ever had.

When the Congress ended, the Graham team invited Anis to come along on their chartered plane to London. He spent 10 days in England, preaching and giving his testimony in several churches. Then he was offered another free trip—this time to New York. It seemed such a miracle, for the Lord had provided passage all the way to the States, and it had cost him nothing.

He arrived with only $65 in his pocket. Immediately doors began opening. He preached in New York City, then churches in Washington, D.C., Virginia, Maryland, Tennessee, North Carolina, Florida, Georgia, and all across the Gulf Coast to Texas. Invitations came also from Monterrey and Mexico City, but Mexico refused to grant a visa on his Jordanian passport.

As more and more opportunities came for him to preach, and the time away from his family grew, Anis began to wonder if perhaps he should make his headquarters in America instead of Jerusalem as he had planned. This problem continued to plague him while he was in Baton Rouge, Louisiana during the middle of December 1966. Then, on the 18th, during his regular morning Bible reading, the words of Acts 22:18 leaped at him from the page. "Make haste, and get thee quickly out of Jerusalem."

Was this really a message from the Lord, or just a coincidence? He read further, "Depart: for I will send thee far hence unto the Gentiles." Could it be the admonition given to the Apostle Paul long before was also a warning to him?

"Lord, let me know Your will," he prayed. "If these words are really meant for me, give me some indication of it this day."

Later that evening, on a flight to his next engagement, Anis had an opportunity to witness to the young man who was his seatmate. After a lengthy discussion the penitent stranger bowed his head and prayed to receive Christ. When he raised his eyes he gave Anis a big smile and said, "You should leave Jerusalem and make your headquarters in the United States."

Anis could feel the hair on the back of his neck standing on end. He had said nothing to the young man about this possibility. The message must have come from God, he decided, and he sent a telegram to Nell that night telling her to come to the States.

Now that the decision was made Anis happily anticipated being reunited with his family. It would be a relief to have them away from the political situation that seemed so explosive. The expected telegram came on Christmas Eve, but instead of a time of arrival it read: "NOT COMING TOO EXPENSIVE MERRY CHRISTMAS."

Nell had misunderstood the message; she thought he wanted them to come for a visit. Anis took time to tape-record a message explaining that he felt the Lord wanted them to make their home in the States. "Sell the furniture and whatever else you can't bring on the plane or ship easily, give the rest away, and come as quickly as possible," he said.

On January 25, 1967 just before Anis was to speak in the large Ruhama Baptist Church in Birmingham, a telegram came advising that Nell and the three boys would land in New York the next day. The three months they had been apart seemed like three years. After speaking, he spent the rest of the night getting to New York and was there for a joyful reunion when they deplaned.

After a couple of days of relaxation, they returned to Alabama and rented a furnished apartment near Nell's folks. Within a week Anis was off for his next revival; he held 14 in seven states during the next four months.

In every town he was treated as a celebrity. Reporters found the "man from Nazareth" intriguingly different from other revivalists. A South Carolina writer described him as "handsome enough to qualify for the 'Sheik of Arabi' role," and "forceful, formidable, and fascinating . . ." The article continued: "He seems to have a way of reading minds and rendering souls bare to scrutiny. So strong is this extra sense people say they feel it in waves. When told of this he quickly said, 'No, this power belongs to anyone, anyone at all who spends enough time with God.'"

In June Anis was invited by Pastor Adrian Rogers to speak at the Merritt Island Baptist Church in the shadow of Cape Kennedy on Florida's east coast. He astounded them by predicting another war would break out soon in the Middle East and Israel would win. Next morning newscasts reported Israeli and Egyptian troops locked in combat. As fighting broke out on other fronts, Anis was besieged by radio and television stations asking about the prospects for peace.

"Peace," he predicted, "will never come to the Bible lands until the Prince of Peace returns. Arabs and Jews will never be reconciled apart from the redeeming love of Jesus."

When the terrifying six days of fighting were over, hundreds of Jordanians and many Egyptians, Syrians, and Israelis had been killed. Israel was now in control of territory from the slopes of Mt. Hermon in the north to the southernmost reaches of the Sinai Peninsula, plus the Gaza Strip and all of the west bank of the Jordan, which included Jerusalem. All of Anis' relatives were safe, but the Baptist church in Old Jerusalem was now in Israeli territory.

Convinced that they should stay in Alabama, they began praying about a home in the Mobile area. They were driving along a freeway one day when Nell noticed a sign on a furniture store advertising a sale. "Let's just look," she suggested. "If we're going to buy a house, we'll need some furniture."

While "just looking" they made friends with the store's Christian owners, Marshall and Betty Campbell, and selected over a thousand dollars worth of furniture. Mr. Campbell called his credit company and said, "I've never asked you for a favor before, and you probably won't believe this, but there's something about this guy. I trust him. Even though he has no house and no credit, I believe he will pay for the furniture in 90 days as he says."

This endorsement got them the furniture and in two weeks they moved into their own home—their first. While Anis was gone for revivals, Nell stayed busy fixing up the house, keeping up with the boys, and doing the office work that kept growing as Anis acquired more friends in the churches where he preached. The office work finally became so extensive that the Campbells gave space in the furniture store for a real office.

In 1968 Anis truly became a world evangelist. He started in January with a crusade in Hong Kong, moved on to Bangkok, then held three major campaigns in West Pakistan. In February he "invaded" India, then the Arab sheikdoms of Kuwait and Bahrain. Even though he spoke through interpreters in many places, he always learned a few words and a song in the local language so he could greet the people and sing for them.

In America Anis preached in the robes and *keffiya* of his homeland at least once in each series of revival meetings. He found, however, that the peoples in the third world identified with him much more when he wore his native attire. At the request of some pastors he began wearing his Arab clothes all the time.

A sampling from some of his letters to Nell is very revealing:

Jan. 15, Karachi: Glorious days. Amazing are His blessings. People here being saved in every service. Yesterday, Sunday, no less than 90 people made public profession.

Jan. 19, Lahore: Wish I were 100 Anises. One to stay with you; the others to preach over the world. Invitations have come like rain. Even here they plead, "Can't you stay longer?" If I do say yes, I'll never get back home.

O, my dearest dear, you have a tremendous reward. David initiated the system of sharing half the spoils with the ones who stay by the stuff. I love you. What more can I say.

Jan. 26, Rawalpindi: Best news is the over 1,000 nightly crowd with 99 decisions first night, then 80, and last night 74. Counseling is given immediately.

Jan. 30, Rawalpindi: So glorious till we couldn't keep up with the decisions—maybe 350 or 400. Attendance was close to 2,000 which meant many stood. I was almost mobbed as dozens surrounded me for a prayer, handshake, or autograph. A youth said, "Even King Hussein didn't get such a reception." I was touched by their faith.

At farewell tea in my honor many words were shared of God's blessings and the smashing success of the campaign.

Feb. 6, Bombay: I am convinced that the Lord did send me to Pakistan. The hundreds of newborn Christians—the greatest single victory is the healing of the terrible breach and dissention among the Christian leaders. Sunday services were packed. People sat on little rugs on cold floors. Not even standing room. About 200 remained after the last message for prayer and counseling. Dr. Khair Ullah, the president of Murray College, drove me to Lahore for the flight. There were more friends to see me off with garlands. The same was repeated in Karachi with gifts and greetings and pleas to come back.

Feb. 16, Gantour, South India: Honey, dear, you would have thought of Pentecost over again. His power of conviction of sin, weeping and shaking and prostrate before Jesus. Such power was available till finally every one present was on his knees. Hundreds trusted the Lord. God's Holy Spirit overpowered everyone.

They asked me to please stay till Sunday. Everywhere I go my heart is touched as they plead stay longer please. "God sent you" is a recurring statement.

Feb. 19, Calcutta: I have never seen such poverty, disease, and ignorance. On the way to hotel in a rickshaw pulled by bicycle we passed many miserable souls who were sleeping on sidewalks by the dozens. One place at least 45 were lined next to each other with hardly room to roll over. In the restaurant when I left rice in my plate the pastor reached out and ate it. There were three others with us, but it did not matter to him.

Dramatic is His power in many instances. Their eagerness

that I pray for them as they kneel in reverence defies any description. I guess they think of me as a holy man, having come from Jerusalem.

Anis arrived home from this first round-the-world trip on March 13 with empty pockets. Travel expenses had been paid with the $1,000 received from the Baptist Mission in Jordan for the station wagon and $1,200 from their long-time supporters the James Cooks and the Paul Cockrells. When Nell told him they had only $6 in the bank, his response was, "Praise the Lord! Some people don't even have one dollar to put in a bank."

God supplied within the week through a friend in North Carolina, who sent a $75 check. Then Anis was off to preach in Jackson, Mississippi.

He was preaching in Texas when Senator Robert Kennedy was assassinated by Sirhan Sirhan, a Palestinian refugee. Anis wept and called it a "shame, a tragedy, a disgrace." Then he told the congregation, "Here, but for the grace of God, stands another Sirhan Sirhan. As a young man I too knew the hopelessness and frustration that has plagued many people for so many years now. Before I met Christ, if I had had the opportunity, I would have done the same thing.

"What that young man and other terrorists are trying to say to the world is this: 'Look at us! We are people. We are Arab Palestinians driven from our lands. Don't just try to pretend we are not here.' The Palestinians are seeking in a pitiful, desperate, terrible way to shake the world awake to the plight of their people. They feel that by giving their lives in fatalistic, suicidal acts they are at least making their deaths count for something.

"Pray for my people. Pray that they may be liberated from their years of exile, but pray most of all that they may find the spiritual liberation that comes to those who know Christ Jesus as Lord and Saviour."

Anis continued preaching across the United States, six or seven revivals in a row, then coming home for a few days to be with his family, rest, and catch up on office work.

He was fulfilling the ministry committed to him. He was an evangelist for the Gospel of Jesus Christ.

Anis, Pastor Ibrahim Awaise (le
Damascus, Syria, and layman E
Khoury (right) of Banyas, Syria
discuss with Billy Graham the
possibility of holding a Congre
Evangelism in Beirut, Lebanon
1972. (Picture was taken at the
Congress on Evangelism in
Amsterdam, Netherlands, 1971

Anis in native dress with singers Phil and Louie
Palermo at the Congress on Evangelism in
Amsterdam,

158

Anis witnessing to the Maharaja
of Hyderabad, India (with
bodyguard in the background),
1971.

Anis in native attire preaching in Chandigarh, Punjab,
India, interpreted by J. James, 1975.

Part of the crowd of 11,000 that heard Anis at the Police Park Stadium near Madras,
India, 1971.

Choirs of the First Baptist Church, Merritt Island, Florida on tour in Jerusalem after the Yom Kippur War, November 1973. Anis is in front, far left (standing).

Anis Shorrosh, American citizen, after the oath was administered by Judge Seybourne Lynne, Mobile, Alabama, July 1972.

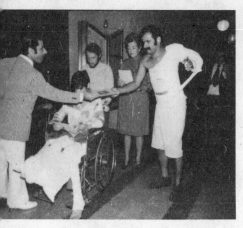

Anis, the Palestinian Arab, ministering to wounded Israeli soldiers, Hadassah Hospital, after the Yom Kippur War, November 1973. "I love you because of Jesus," was his message.

Willem van der Hoeven, one-time keeper of Garden Tomb, Jerusalem, preaching in the rden of Gethsemane, January 1975. Van der even's prophecy is that Anis will be used ghtily by God among both Jews and Arabs in days to come.

161

The Anis Shorrosh family

16
THE PROPHECY

One day in late 1968, in the furniture store office, Betty Campbell asked, "Anis, do you know anyone who would take us to the Holy Land?"

"Sure," he replied, grinning. "Me."

Three days later he came into the store and said, "Where's the money?"

"Money?" Betty repeated. "What money?"

"For your trip to the Holy Land. I've already made the arrangements." When Betty and Marshall saw what a good deal he had worked out, they decided to include their two daughters. Others friends asked to join the tour and by departure time 18 were set to go. Since Anis was the tour director, Nell could go free.

Anis was a little apprehensive since it would be his first time in 20 years to travel in the territory now controlled by Israel. He wasn't certain how they would accept him as an Arab. He thought that since he was leading a tour of "pilgrims," the Israelis would not interfere. They were not known to be unfriendly to American tourist dollars.

Everything went smoothly. Visas were issued without question. When they arrived, Israeli customs officers passed them through with smiles. Anis preached to a packed house in the church he had once pastored and embraced many old friends who were now subjects of Israel. Then on to Bethlehem, Mt. Carmel, Capernaum, and the green hills of Galilee. At last they entered the town of Nazareth.

Once more Anis climbed the hill to his grandmother's home outside the city. She hugged and kissed him with tears streaming down her furrowed cheeks, then turned to embrace Nell. Then as any hospitable Arab woman would do, she invited him to bring in the entire busload of tourists and served everyone coffee, tea, and cakes.

As their tour bus drew near the home his father had built, Anis grew quiet and thoughtful. Nell knew him well enough by this time to understand that when he was affected deeply about something, he said nothing. The bus stopped, then Anis got out and walked to the home in which he had grown up. The trees were much larger, but other than that everything looked so familiar that it was hard to believe he had not seen it in over 20 years. He saw that the house was occupied. He thought of how his mother had never received a cent of rent or other compensation since the house was confiscated. It was unfair and unjust, but by the grace of God he held no bitterness. He turned and walked quietly back to the bus, too choked to speak.

That night he spoke at the Baptist mission church he had attended as a boy. He was amazed to find that the building he remembered so well was not nearly as large as he had thought. It was jammed that night with former friends and relatives filling the main floor and all three of the small balconies that surrounded the chapel. How they sang and praised God for His goodness that night. It was a grand homecoming and an emotion-packed experience for Anis.

Marshall Campbell had brought along a movie camera to film the archaeological and historical sights of the trip as background for a movie about the life of Christ. When they returned to Alabama, Anis spent days, and often nights, in the Campbells' dining room, editing and splicing film. When the editing was all done and the film timed for 28 minutes, a Mobile television station ran it. Calls came from churches, old folks' homes, and colleges in four states asking to see it.

The next year, 1969, brought more revivals and invitations from the Far East begging Anis to make return visits. Marshall Campbell agreed to accompany him as far as the Middle East so they might shoot footage for movie documentaries about Jordan, Lebanon, and Egypt. The mayor of Mobile, Lambert Mims, commissioned Anis as a goodwill ambassador and gave him keys to the city to present to the heads of state in the various countries he would visit.

For a while Anis wondered if he would get to present any of the keys, for after filming scenes in Tyre and Sidon they were stopped by angry Lebanese soldiers.

"Did you take pictures of that bridge?" a harsh voice demanded.

"Why, yes, we did," Anis replied.

"That is a military target. You are under arrest."

"But, Sergeant, we are men of peace," Anis explained, getting from the car to talk with the soldiers. "We meant no harm."

"Men have been killed for less."

"But I am a goodwill ambassador from the United States. See this golden key?" he asked, fishing it from his pocket to display for the wide-eyed soldiers. "Tomorrow I am to present this to your president on behalf of the people in Mobile, Alabama."

The sergeant swallowed hard, snapped to attention, and gave Anis a crisp military salute. "Well, Mr. Ambassador," he said nervously, "you should be proud of us for doing our job so well."

"Yes," Anis agreed. "You are doing an excellent job. Carry on."

He dashed back to the car. "Get moving!" he ordered the driver, while smiling at the soldiers and waving good-bye.

After they were a safe distance down the road, Anis let out a long sigh and told Marshall calmly, "Perhaps we should be a little more discreet about what we decide to film in the future."

The next day Anis presented the greatly prized key to the president of Lebanon. Others he gave to King Hussein of Jordan, the governors of Bombay and Mysore, and to Pastor Daniel Chung of the Baptist church of Hong Kong. As he was welcomed into the mansions and palaces of political rulers he shared his testimony and gave each a Bible.

The crowds on the Indian subcontinent were even greater than before. At one place over 2,000 jammed into the church with a thousand more standing on cars, walls, and rooftops to see. When Anis came to preach he had to enter the church through a window!

There was so much interest in this trip among supporters back in the States that Anis decided to publish a book about it. *An Ambassador for Jesus* seemed the perfect title. But when the world traveler returned home he found there was only $13 in the family bank account. "Well, praise the Lord!" he told Nell again. "We've had more than a 100-percent increase since last time."

During the next few days their meager funds dwindled. One evening Anis went to preach in a church. They took an offering, but gave him a check for the amount given. Anis accepted the check with an embarrassed look on his face. When the pastor asked him what was wrong, he confessed, "I don't have money for gas to get home."

As Anis' evangelistic work continued to grow, his friends suggested that it would be best to establish a legal, non-profit evangelistic association. Contributions would be tax deductible. Any criticism of profiteering by Anis and Nell would be prevented. And the Shorroshes would be paid a moderate, but regular salary.

So in October 1970 the Anis Shorrosh Evangelistic Association was incorporated and dedicated to the preaching of revival crusades around the world, supporting national workers, providing Bible-centered cassettes, sponsoring international students, publishing Christian books, producing documentary films, and leading annual Holy Land pilgrimages.

Anis was named president; Dr. Jim Cook, vice-president; Marshall Campbell, treasurer; and Dr. Gene Keebler, secretary. Several other long-time friends agreed to serve as board members.

So many invitations kept coming from India that Anis realized it would take six months to accept them all. He certainly did not want to be away from his family that long, and the Association could not afford to fly him home every two months for a visit. His board members agreed with him that it would be best to take Nell and the boys along.

They went by way of Jordan, stopped at the Ajlun hospital to see missionary friends, then motored on to Irbid to visit Anis' family and relatives.

Once they rode by the sprawling refugee camp near Irbid. The people were still there, vacant-eyed and listless, a painful, continuing testimony to the failure of over two decades of resolutions and negotiations. In comparison, India's problems seemed more solvable.

They made beautiful Bangalore in humid South India their headquarters. Salam, 11, was enrolled in school, but because of the expense Nell decided to teach Paul, 9, and Stevie, 7, using the Calvert Course. She also helped in the Baptist clinic, so was kept quite busy as Anis traveled to crusades in major cities around the populous country.

After a few months Anis decided he would have to have a talk with his wife about a very delicate matter. He found it hard to believe, but his well-disciplined wife was gaining weight. In India, with so much hunger all around them, he felt this was a bad testimony.

"Nell," he began as tactfully as he could, "I want you to promise me that when we leave India you will not weigh more than when we came."

"I'm afraid I can't do that."

"Oh yes you can. I have great confidence in you. You can do it."

"Not when I'm pregnant."

Anis blinked. He sat there staring with his mouth open. Nell began to giggle. For the first time since she had met him Anis was absolutely speechless. He just couldn't believe that after 13 years of marriage he could be so naive as not to have realized her condition before.

"Why didn't you tell me?" he asked finally.

"Well, I just wanted to see how long it would take for you to catch on," she replied, enjoying his shock.

He sat there shaking his head in disbelief. They had decided they couldn't afford any more children. He had never thought about a "surprise" baby. But now that one was coming . . .

"It will be a girl," he decided. "And since 'Victory in Jesus' is our theme song for this crusade, we'll name her Victoria."

Nell just smiled. Her pregnancy had made it very difficult to adjust to the hot climate and the spicy curry they were served everywhere, but she was determined to miss nothing during their time in India. Between crusades the family went to see the Taj Mahal and other famous monuments of the past. They also had an audience at the presidential palace with President V. V. Giri. The president graciously accepted the key to Mobile from Anis and listened politely to his testimony. After Anis had prayed for the president and for India, they were given a tour of the palace gardens. As they were about to leave, the gracious host surprised Nell by presenting her with a gorgeous bouquet of roses.

While Anis was in India, the Lord enabled him to complete and publish his third book, *Ultimate Reality,* an exposition of seven basic Christian doctrines.

When their six months were over, Indian church leaders thanked Anis profusely. Thousands of Indians, they reported, had become Christians under his preaching. "You give the lie to those who say Christianity is just the western white man's religion," one said.

Back in Mobile they found invitations for revivals in the U.S. were stacked up. Anis was in Texas when Victoria Anis was born. No planes were flying because of electrical storms, and he did not get to greet his beautiful daughter till she was four days old. She captivated his heart immediately. The natural born charmer soon made adoring subjects of her three older brothers as well as her parents.

Invitations came from the Far East begging Anis to return. Anis decided to take another tour group to the Holy Land; this would make it possible for him to make another preaching trip around the world. Since Nell would have to stay home with little Victoria, Anis chose Dr. Gene Keebler, his old friend and mentor from Clarke College days, to be his roommate.

He realized his folly their first night together in Israel. Gene snored. He really snored. Anis was exhausted from the long flight, and had to preach the next morning. He was so desperate for sleep that he dragged his mattress into the bathroom and shoved it into the bathtub.

A short while later Gene awoke, discovered Anis missing, and found him sleeping soundly in the bathtub.

"What in the world?" Gene exclaimed.

"You snore so loud, I can't sleep."

"I'm sorry, I made you do this," the educator said sheepishly. "But I have some sleeping pills. Take half of one and that should help you sleep."

"Well, I don't know," Anis protested. "I've never taken sleeping pills. I don't like taking pills."

"Oh, come on. Half a pill couldn't harm you."

Anis swallowed the medication. It worked. Too well. The next morning Gene called him without response. He shook him and still Anis did not stir.

Then Gene began to panic. Not that he feared Anis was ill, but he surely couldn't preach in Arabic. The guide came and they walked Anis around, filled him with coffee, and finally, about nine o'clock, the "sleeper" was able to stagger up to the pulpit and preach.

After the service Anis was wide awake and able to joke about the incident. As they were leaving for lunch, he nudged Gene and said, "No offense, Man, but I prefer Nell for a roommate."

After the tour of the Holy Land the group returned to the states, but Anis traveled on to India and Pakistan. After the successful crusades there he came home by way of Holland, where he participated in the European Congress on Evangelism, and Germany, where he held a short crusade.

After returning home he made a decision he had long been deliberating. He applied for U.S. citizenship. He received his citizenship, not as the spouse of a citizen, but on his own merit as an evangelist with religious priority status. This would make it easier to get visas into some countries.

The group tours and evangelistic crusades abroad had now become annual affairs. One of the most gripping experiences of Anis' life occurred on one of his visits to Israel. Their bus was heading north through the green fields of Galilee toward his hometown of Nazareth. The Jewish tour guide sat next to Anis on the front seat of the air-conditioned bus as they barreled past long rows of huge cabbages.

The guide turned to Anis and casually remarked, "I was a captain in the tank force that occupied Nazareth back in '48."

The announcement made Anis' flesh crawl. "You what?" he asked, wanting to make certain he had heard correctly.

"I was a captain in the tank force in '48. We took the town of Nazareth," he repeated a little apprehensively as he noticed the expression on Anis' face. Something about the glint in Anis' eyes made him realize for the first time how very Arab this American looked.

Sounds seemed to explode in Anis' brain. He could hear once again the terrifying blast of the tanks' cannons. The screams of terror as the villagers ran for cover. The fearful sobs of the group huddled in the dark cave.

His eyes narrowed and his nostrils flared in indignation as he remembered the look of panic on his mother's face as she gathered her children to her. He thought of Abu Suhail and his father. His father. Lying somewhere in an unmarked grave.

Anis took a deep breath and slowly, fighting to keep his voice under control, said, "My father was killed in the battle of Nazareth."

The blue-eyed Israeli looked Anis straight in the eye. His muscles tensed as he waited to see what action the Palestinian might take.

All the hate-filled passions of his youth seemed to flow once again through Anis' veins. How many times had he longed for an opportunity to avenge his father's death? The wild plans he had made with his friends. The bloody plots he had devised to repay the despicable enemy that had forced his family from their home.

And here sat the very man who had led the attack. Never in his most fanciful daydreams had he ever imagined he would meet this individual. He didn't look so tough. The adrenalin was surging through Anis' body so strongly that he had no doubt he could overpower the man.

"My father was killed in Nazareth," Anis repeated. "And by all the tradition and the tribal laws of my people it is my duty to avenge his death."

But then an overwhelming love enveloped Anis, and with a voice that seemed to belong to Someone else, he solemnly announced, "But because Jesus Christ of Nazareth has forgiven my sins, I forgive you."

This unexpected reply so shook the guide that he didn't quite know how to respond. He had been ready to justify his deeds, but instead said, "I'm sorry. Very sorry. I had no way of knowing . . . There were very few people killed."

"It may have seemed few to you. I not only lost my father, but a very dear cousin was killed by a machine gunner who pumped so many bullets into his body he was nearly cut in half.

"At one time, I would have gladly taken your life to pay for theirs, but let me tell you about Jesus, who changed me and gave me new life. He can do the same for you."

"We lost men too," the guide inserted, changing the subject. "When we fought the Syrian tanks just before we got to town."

"Syrian tanks?" Anis exclaimed. "You mean the Syrians really did try to help us?"

"Oh, yes. That's how we got the idea of painting Syrian emblems on our tanks."

"I never knew that," Anis commented softly. "You know, it's all too easy to go through life misunderstanding some very important matters . . ." and he turned the conversation back to spiritual concerns.

This wasn't the first or the last opportunity Anis had to share Christ with a Jew, but it convinced him that he had truly forgiven those responsible for the death of his loved ones.

An even more dramatic opportunity to share Christ with those who were supposed to be his enemies came soon after the Yom Kippur War in 1973. The choirs from the First Baptist Church of Merritt Island, Florida were touring the Holy Land with Anis, and had been invited to entertain wounded Israeli soldiers at Hadassah Hospital, the largest Jewish medical center in the world.

First, the vocal choir presented selections from the Broadway musical, "Fiddler on the Roof." The Hebrew boys loved the music and clapped loudly. Then the handbell choir made merry with traditional Christmas music. Now it was Anis' time to speak.

He stood gazing at the battered forms of the brave young men. There was a handsome lieutenant who had lost an eye and both legs. Others in wheelchairs had limbs missing. A few were in traction in their beds. All looked at him expectantly. He was well aware that the moment he spoke they would recognize from his accent that he was an Arab.

"My name is Anis Shorrosh," he began. "I was born in this country many years before any of you. My father was killed during your first war of independence and I was filled with hatred toward your people. But one day when I was 18, something happened in my life. I found peace through Jesus Christ, my Messiah. Very humbly I tell you tonight . . . I love you because of Jesus. And I pray for peace."

He waited anxiously after each sentence as his words were translated into Hebrew. The young soldiers all listened attentively, then called out, "We love you because of Moses!"

The laughter that filled the room melted the icy wall that had come between them. Jews and Arabs, all descendants of Abraham, communicating respect for one another. The service was a healing balm to the young Jewish soldiers. A healing of bitterness.

The significance of this event, and possibly the whole of Anis Shorrosh's life is perhaps understood best by his spirit-brother, Jan Willem van der Hoeven. Jan Willem has prophesied:

"The Lord has a great purpose for Anis Shorrosh. Few Arabs have the openness toward Israel that he has. I believe the Lord is going to send a great revival to the Middle East. It may come after another war when the shock of the bloodshed will be so terrible there will be an openness among Arabs and Jews alike. But the only hope of reconciliation is in Christ. It just could be that Anis is God's man for the task. It will be interesting to see what God does through him in the future. Pray for him."

Update—1984

A decade has passed since the writing of *The Liberated Palestinian.*

Another decade of fighting, bombing, terrorism, suicide attacks, and killing of the innocent in the land of the Bible where Anis Shorrosh was born.

For Anis, these have been exciting, dynamic, and challenging years, during which he has gained world renown as an evangelist. To some, "Palestinian" symbolizes terrorist; to others, heroic fighter; to still others, pitiful refugee. For the thousands who have heard him, this Palestinian, himself a former refugee, is an apostle of love and forgiveness.

His major ministry has been in the United States, yet in Muslim Pakistan he is perhaps the best known and most respected of all Christian leaders. In one series of meetings some 2500 Pakistanis made commitments to Christ after hearing him preach. A Christian lay leader in Rawalpindi, a major urban center, told him, "Half of all the Christians in our city became believers under your ministry."

In India he drew such large crowds that anti-Christian elements worked to have his visa revoked.

In Guyana, South America, twelve thousand people turned out to hear him, with over nine hundred making public decisions for Christ. A Jewish Christian directed the music for his crusade there. Said the Jew: "Only Christ can make a Jew love an Arab." Replied Anis: "Yes, and only Christ can make an Arab love a Jew!"

He has preached and led revivals in hundreds of churches in the United States, from Alaska to Florida, for congregations numbering less than one hundred to over five thousand. Many of these churches baptized more converts than in any previous revival crusade. Pastor Ferrel Mills of Faith Baptist Church, Anchorage, the largest Southern Baptist Church in Alaska, reported that "our crowds were three times larger with Anis than when we had the president of our denomination."

Thousands upon thousands have discovered the transforming power of Christ through his ministry. Among them is a Louisiana man who had killed two people while driving drunk. Five weeks later, this man and his wife heard the message of love from Anis. Both accepted Christ in their home. That evening when Anis gave the invitation in the church for public professions of faith, they came forward, the wife pushing her injured husband in a wheel chair. The widow, whose husband and son were killed in the crash, tearfully told the congregation. "God has answered our prayers. I hold no grudges against this man because of Jesus' love."

Anis' example of forgiving his former enemies has brought many opportunities to witness to Jews. One day he was getting off a plane at the Mobile, Alabama, airport and spotted a passenger who looked familiar.

The man was, as Anis thought, former Israeli Defense Minister Ezer Weizman. When Anis called his name, Weizman tensed. He was traveling incognito and was surprised at being recognized. When Anis identified himself as a Palestinian, the former Israeli official instinctively froze. Anis just smiled at him and said. "I'm a Palestinian who loves the Jews because I love Jesus, and I've got a gift for you."

As Anis reached into his briefcase, the distinguished Jew still looked apprehensive. Then he forced a smile as he saw the Palestinian extending only a book. It was Anis' *Jesus, Prophecy, and the Middle East.* Anis autographed the book and they departed as friends.

After one of the numerous pilgrimages Anis made to the Holy Lands a very shocking letter arrived to his home. It was from his good friend, Dr. Ray Register. The Baptist Missionary, who serves in Nazareth and the Galilee area, related in the letter how a terrorist confessed to planting two bombs on two different buses in Jerusalem. Only one of the bombs exploded injuring the passengers and causing some fatalities. The terrorist was mystified why the other never exploded.

Upon some speedy investigations of the color and type of bus, the demolition squad found the bomb which had been under the bus for weeks. The bus was in Nazareth and it was one of the Galilee buses Anis had used for two weeks. Nell, trembled as she read the letter. "You're not going to tell people about this are you?" she declared. "They would certainly be scared to death to come with us on our next tour!" Anis replied, "If God would shut the mouth of lions for Daniel in the lions den, He can certainly diffuse a bomb for His servant Anis Shorrosh."

An article in the "Birmingham News" appeared Jan. 8, 1978 entitled, "Did Alabamian's life in Palestine influence Carter?"

The writer, author of five books and currently president of the Alabama Baptist Convention, put forth a very remarkable theory concerning Shorrosh's influence on the peace treaty between Egypt and Israel. Wallace Henley related how the President was given a copy of *The Liberated Palestinian* and soon after that direct statements concerning the Palestinians began to appear in his speeches.

While holding revivals in major cities, Anis is a "natural" for media interviews and profiles. Many reporters have been personally touched by his testimony of "the love God has given me for the Jews." One Jewish T.V. interviewer in Tucson, Arizona, was in tears as Anis described his experience on camera.

Anis is often told by Jews, especially in Israel, "We wish all the Arabs were like you." But when the Palestinian presents Jesus, they shrug and say, "We've got our Moses and you have your Jesus."

However, Anis has found a few Jews in Israel to be secret believers in Jesus as their Messiah—perhaps as many as 5000. One, a highly placed government official, said, "Anis, if all the Jews and Arabs believed like us, we would have peace."

As a dedicated Bible student, Anis finds Biblical promises that apply to both Arabs and Jews. He sees the state of Israel as a fulfillment of Biblical prophecy, but maintains that Israel has "pushed its advantage too far in continued occupation of the West Bank and in taking property from some Palestinians and Lebanese without just compensation.

He also holds that "evangelical Christians in America tend to ignore problems in the land of the Bible and wait for the fulfillment of prophecy. "We must deal with present situations, particularly the Palestinian problem," he urges, "Over two million of my people are suffering. Many are bitter, sick, and lonely. Some have been in refugee camps for over 35 years."

So Anis supports "a small Palestinian state with its own police force, but without a standing army, on the West Bank."

To some of his Arab friends who press for more fighting with Israel, he answers, "bullets have not brought peace, but the Bible will. Guns have not solved our problems, only the Gospel of Jesus can ever stop hatred and bloodshed. Jesus didn't say on the cross, 'Father, Kill Them,' but 'Father, Forgive Them.' "

In his meetings, Anis prefers not to speak on sensitive political issues. "I am an ambassador of the King of kings and Lord of lords," he declares. "I bear His message of love and forgiveness."

The Anis Shorrosh Evangelistic Association continues to back him in this mission. Leaders of the Association have loyally stood by him through his years as an evangelist. It stands as a tribute to Anis and a testimony of their confidence in him that there has never been any cleavage in the Association.

All offerings received from revivals and income from books, cassettes, films, etc. goes into the Association treasury, from which the evangelist is paid a salary. Financial statements are available to contributors, but sent quarterly to Board Members.

Association members contribute both money and time to the ministry of their evangelist. Some have accompanied him on evangelistic trips overseas and assisted with preaching and personal witnessing.

For many years the Association has provided financial support for a number of international students and a select group of Christian workers in Israel, Jordan, Lebanon, India, Pakistan, Sri Lanka, and Nepal. The students are enrolled in colleges, medical schools, seminaries and Bible schools in the United States and abroad.

Examples of "alumni," supported as students by the Association include the following:

—Tawfiq Batarseh, from Jordan, graduated from New Orleans Baptist Theological Seminary and is now married to a Mississippian and pastoring a church in Meridian, Miss. Tawfiq has also served a church in Jordan.

—Dr. Mobin Khan, from Varanasi, India, holds two earned doctorates, including a doctorate in missiology from Fuller Theological Seminary. He carries on a ministry among Muslims in California.

—Fawzi Shorrosh, graduated from Clarke Junior College and Mobile Baptist College. He served as an evangelist for four years and is now pastor of a Baptist church in Mississippi.

—Mona Sayegh, was saved during a bus ride in Galilee while Anis was leading an American tour group to the Holy Land in 1976. Mona graduated in pre-medicine from Mobile College. He is now completing studies in medical technology at Anderson, South Carolina, and serves on occasions as a soloist in evangelistic crusades.

—John Ishmael, whose father served as Anis' interpreter during several missionary trips to India, graduated from Allahabad Bible School in India in May, 1983. He now ministers as a Bible teacher and evangelist in central India.

Examples of pastors and evangelists helped by the Association in ministry overseas, include the following:

—George Kazoura, pastor of the Baptist Church in Rama, Israel. The church is now an effective witness in the Galilee area among Arabs and Jews, where Jesus performed eighty percent of his miracles.

—T. T. Varghese, has served faithfully and successfully as an evangelist in Cochin and other parts of South India for the past fourteen years under the sole sponsorship of the Shorrosh Evangelistic Association.

—Dr. B A. Prabahker heads the Asia For Christ organization in Secunderabad, India. The Association supports twelve native evangelists through Asia For Christ.

—Cedric Atkinson of Colombo, Sri Lanka, felt God's call to the ministry in 1979. He and his bride were sent to India where they graduated with a Theological degree May, 1984.

Twice yearly, Anis leads a pilgrimage to his native Holy Land. A "must" stop is always Nazareth where he never tires of showing American friends the roads where Jesus walked and the places dear to his own childhood.

Anis' home remains in Mobile where in 1984 he and his "sweetheart" are celebrating their 27th wedding anniversary. Nell joins him for occasional revivals and on most Holy Land pilgrimages. At home she has nobly and sacrificially given herself to parenting, while her globe-trotting husband is away. She also serves as an organist in their local church and as the financial secretary for the organization.

For Nell and Anis, the "nest" has been emptying too fast. Salam, their eldest, recently received his degree in marketing from Samford (Baptist) University in Birmingham, Alabama. He is now employed in Mobile. Paul is studying for the ministry at West Palm Beach Atlantic College in Florida, where Anis and Nell's close friend, Dr. Gene Keebler is vice-president. Steve, their youngest son, employed by Southwest Airlines and committed to the ministry of evangelism, attends the Criswell Center for Biblical Studies in Dallas, Texas. Victoria, the youngest, is a star student in the seventh grade and according to her father, "also plays the piano and sings beautifully."

"Em Assad," Anis' beloved mother, continues to live in Jordan. However, Anis and Nell are working with immigration authorities to bring her to their home permanently.

Assad, Anis' older brother, is an oil executive in Houston, Texas.

Samuel, the younger brother, is a bank employee in a town near Irbid, Jordan. Kamleh, Anis' sister, lives with her husband and three of their six children in Mobile. The married three include a medical doctor, an optometrist, and an engineer. They were assisted in their education by the Anis Shorrosh Evangelistic Association.

It has been thirty-six years since the Shorrosh family left Nazareth for refuge in Jordan. At that time no one would have predicted that one of the sons would become a world-renowned evangelist, author of six books and producer of five motion picture documentaries. Or that he would earn four academic degrees, including the Doctor of Ministry, earned at Luther Rice International Seminary in Jacksonville, Florida. But then, in the words of a Gospel chorus which Dr. Anis Shorrosh has taught multitudes to sing: "Who can tell what God can do! Who can tell His love for you! In the name of Jesus, Jesus, we have the victory."